FLORA WILSON BROWN

Flora Wilson Brown is a writer and dramaturg. She is a co-founder of DONOTALIGHT, a theatre company interested in new writing about living in the world today and telling political stories through a personal lens. DONOTALIGHT produced her first play *I Know I Know I Know* (directed by co-founder Harry Tennison) at the Southwark Playhouse in 2022 to critical acclaim. Her second play, *The Beautiful Future is Coming*, was first presented for a short run at the Jermyn Street Theatre as part of their 2024 Footprints Festival, also directed by Tennison. Flora has also written a musical for families with Intrepid Fools, *Viking*, which was presented at Underbelly for Edinburgh Fringe 2019. She is currently working on a variety of projects for stage and screen.

Other Titles in this Series

Chris Bush
THE ASSASSINATION OF KATIE HOPKINS
 with Matt Winkworth
THE CHANGING ROOM
CHRIS BUSH PLAYS: ONE
A DOLL'S HOUSE *after* Ibsen
FAUSTUS: THAT DAMNED WOMAN
HUNGRY
JANE EYRE *after* Brontë
THE LAST NOËL
OTHERLAND
ROBIN HOOD AND THE
 CHRISTMAS HEIST
 with Matt Winkworth
ROCK / PAPER / SCISSORS
STANDING AT THE SKY'S EDGE
 with Richard Hawley
STEEL

Jez Butterworth
THE FERRYMAN
THE HILLS OF CALIFORNIA
JERUSALEM
JEZ BUTTERWORTH PLAYS: ONE
JEZ BUTTERWORTH PLAYS: TWO
MOJO
THE NIGHT HERON
PARLOUR SONG
THE RIVER
THE WINTERLING

Caryl Churchill
BLUE HEART
CHURCHILL PLAYS: THREE
CHURCHILL PLAYS: FOUR
CHURCHILL PLAYS: FIVE
CHURCHILL: SHORTS
CLOUD NINE
DING DONG THE WICKED
A DREAM PLAY *after* Strindberg
DRUNK ENOUGH TO SAY I LOVE YOU?
ESCAPED ALONE
FAR AWAY
GLASS. KILL. BLUEBEARD'S FRIENDS.
 IMP.
HERE WE GO
HOTEL
ICECREAM
LIGHT SHINING IN BUCKINGHAMSHIRE
LOVE AND INFORMATION
MAD FOREST
A NUMBER
PIGS AND DOGS
SEVEN JEWISH CHILDREN
THE SKRIKER
THIS IS A CHAIR
THYESTES *after* Seneca
TRAPS
WHAT IF IF ONLY

Branden Jacobs-Jenkins
APPROPRIATE
THE COMEUPPANCE
GLORIA
AN OCTOROON

Lucy Kirkwood
BEAUTY AND THE BEAST
 with Katie Mitchell
BLOODY WIMMIN
THE CHILDREN
CHIMERICA
HEDDA *after* Ibsen
THE HUMAN BODY
IT FELT EMPTY WHEN THE HEART
 WENT AT FIRST BUT IT IS
 ALRIGHT NOW
LUCY KIRKWOOD PLAYS: ONE
MOSQUITOES
NSFW
RAPTURE
TINDERBOX
THE WELKIN

Benedict Lombe
LAVA
SHIFTERS

Jack Thorne
2ND MAY 1997
AFTER LIFE *after* Hirokazu Kore-eda
BUNNY
BURYING YOUR BROTHER IN
 THE PAVEMENT
A CHRISTMAS CAROL *after* Dickens
THE END OF HISTORY…
HOPE
JACK THORNE PLAYS: ONE
JACK THORNE PLAYS: TWO
JUNKYARD
LET THE RIGHT ONE IN
 after John Ajvide Lindqvist
THE MOTIVE AND THE CUE
MYDIDAE
THE SOLID LIFE OF SUGAR WATER
STACY & FANNY AND FAGGOT
WHEN WINSTON WENT TO WAR WITH
 THE WIRELESS
WHEN YOU CURE ME
WOYZECK *after* Büchner

debbie tucker green
BORN BAD
DEBBIE TUCKER GREEN PLAYS: ONE
DIRTY BUTTERFLY
EAR FOR EYE
HANG
NUT
A PROFOUNDLY AFFECTIONATE,
 PASSIONATE DEVOTION TO
 SOMEONE (– *NOUN*)
RANDOM
STONING MARY
TRADE & GENERATIONS
TRUTH AND RECONCILIATION

Phoebe Waller-Bridge
FLEABAG

Ross Willis
WOLFIE
WONDER BOY

Flora Wilson Brown

THE BEAUTIFUL FUTURE IS COMING

NICK HERN BOOKS
London
www.nickhernbooks.co.uk

A Nick Hern Book

The Beautiful Future is Coming first published in Great Britain in 2025 as a paperback original by Nick Hern Books Limited, The Glasshouse, 49a Goldhawk Road, London W12 8QP

The Beautiful Future is Coming copyright © 2025 Flora Wilson Brown

Flora Wilson Brown has asserted her moral right to be identified as the author of this work

Cover image: design by Steph Pyne; photography by Michael Wharley

Designed and typeset by Nick Hern Books, London
Printed in the UK by Mimeo Ltd, Huntingdon, Cambridgeshire PE29 6XX

A CIP catalogue record for this book is available from the British Library

ISBN 978 1 83904 439 7

CAUTION All rights whatsoever in this play are strictly reserved. Requests to reproduce the text in whole or in part should be addressed to the publisher. This book may not be used, in whole or in part, for the development or training of artificial intelligence technologies or systems.

Amateur Performing Rights Applications for performance, including readings and excerpts, by amateurs in the English language throughout the world should be addressed to the Performing Rights Department, Nick Hern Books, The Glasshouse, 49a Goldhawk Road, London W12 8QP, *tel* +44 (0)20 8749 4953, *email* rights@nickhernbooks.co.uk, except as follows:

Australia: ORiGiN Theatrical, Level 1, 213 Clarence Street, Sydney NSW 2000, *tel* +61 (2) 8514 5201, *email* enquiries@originmusic.com.au, *web* www.origintheatrical.com.au

New Zealand: Play Bureau, 20 Rua Street, Mangapapa, Gisborne, 4010, *tel* +64 21 258 3998, *email* info@playbureau.com

United States and Canada: Casarotto Ramsay and Associates Ltd, see details below

Professional Performing Rights Applications for performance by professionals in any medium and in any language throughout the world (including by stock companies in the USA and Canada) should be addressed to Casarotto Ramsay and Associates Ltd, *email* rights@casarotto.co.uk, www.casarotto.co.uk

No performance of any kind may be given unless a licence has been obtained. Applications should be made before rehearsals begin. Publication of this play does not necessarily indicate its availability for amateur performance.

www.nickhernbooks.co.uk/environmental-policy

Nick Hern Books' authorised representative in the EU is
Easy Access System Europe – Mustamäe tee 50, 10621 Tallinn, Estonia
email gpsr.requests@easproject.com

This version of *The Beautiful Future is Coming* was first performed at the Bristol Old Vic on 15 May 2025, with the following cast:

MALCOM	James Bradwell
ANA	Rosie Dwyer
DAN	Michael Salami
CLAIRE	Nina Singh
EUNICE	Phoebe Thomas
JOHN	Matt Whitchurch
Director	Nancy Medina
Set & Costume Designer	Aldo Vázquez
Lighting Designer	Ryan Day
Sound Designer	Elena Peña
Composer	Femi Temowo
Casting Director	Sam Jones CDG
Assistant Director	Ignė Barkauskaitė
Costume Supervisor	Sophia Khan

An earlier version of the play was first performed at Jermyn Street Theatre, London, as a part of their 2024 Footprints Festival. The cast was as follows:

JOHN / DAN / MALCOM	George Fletcher
EUNICE	Sabrina Wu
CLAIRE	Martha Watson Allpress
ANA	Pepter Lunkuse
Director	Harry Tennison
Sound Designer	Anna Short
Lighting Designer	Nell Golledge

This play is dedicated to John Wilson

Characters

EUNICE, *New York, 1856*
JOHN, *New York, 1856*
CLAIRE, *London, 2027*
DAN, *London, 2027*
ANA, *Svalbard, 2100*
MALCOM, *Svalbard, 2100*

Notes

/ indicates the point at which the next speaker interrupts; at the start of the line indicates simultaneous speech.

– could be a change in thought, could be a self-correction/silencing, could be that the following line should follow immediately, could be all sorts of things.

Most of this play should happen quickly, apart from when it doesn't.

You can play with beats and pauses and silences. They're just my first thoughts of where those rhythms will fall.

Italics in [*square brackets*] are thoughts that the characters aren't saying.

*

Eunice and John are based on my research about Eunice and Elisha Foote, however some of it is exaggerated or imagined or completely incorrect. This isn't a biography or an attempt at one.

This text went to press before the end of rehearsals and so may differ slightly from the play as performed.

One

There is a moment when the play starts – the three women on stage, they might look at each other.

JOHN *walks in, carrying a letter.*

JOHN. Eunice –

EUNICE *doesn't look up.*

EUNICE. Hm?

JOHN. It's here –

EUNICE. What?

JOHN. From London.

She looks up, he holds out the letter. She opens it. She reads it quickly and puts it down on the table.

What do they –

EUNICE. They won't read it –

JOHN. They won't –

EUNICE (*reading*). 'Although we're sure you consider your findings to be of great importance, the Royal Society can't make a habit of reading every paper by every hobbyist.'

JOHN. I've always thought they were idiots –

EUNICE. The Royal Society, John –

JOHN. They're European –

EUNICE. They're English –

JOHN. That's worse.

EUNICE (*reading again*). 'Perhaps a young woman like yourself should find a more pleasant use for her time – '

JOHN. Stop reading it, Eunice –

EUNICE. We hear lacemaking is very popular in your part of the world.

JOHN. Eunice –

EUNICE. I really thought if they'd just read it –

JOHN. I know –

EUNICE. Just open it and – read it – just read it –

JOHN. But they're not going to –

EUNICE. I know – I know that, John, obviously –

JOHN. I know – I'm sorry –

Pause.

EUNICE. I just – I really thought – I really do think that this one could be important. Could be really –

JOHN. I agree.

EUNICE. I think it could have real – real-world – it could mean something – couldn't it?

JOHN. Absolutely –

EUNICE. I think it's even – even exciting / a little –

JOHN. It is so exciting –

EUNICE. Just – just sunlight and carbonic acid and the temperature rises. Just like that.

JOHN. Just like that.

EUNICE. I wasn't expecting – I don't know – fanfare – but I thought if they'd just – read it.

Beat.

JOHN. I think – it doesn't matter how good it is –

EUNICE. I know, John.

JOHN. And I know you know. I just hate – seeing you like this when they're never –

EUNICE. I know –

JOHN. This is the third time –

EUNICE. I know you think it's a waste of time –

JOHN. I never – Eunice, I never said that. I don't think it's a waste of time – I think you are so brilliant –

EUNICE. Right.

JOHN. I think it's – I think they're stupid – and bigoted –

EUNICE. The *Royal Society*, John.

JOHN. I know. I know – but they're just not – they're not going to –

Pause. CLAIRE *has two takeaway coffees.*

EUNICE. No.

JOHN. I know it's not enough –

EUNICE. John –

JOHN. But I really do – I think you are brilliant.

DAN *runs in.*

Two

CLAIRE. Late again –

DAN. Am I.

CLAIRE. Sixteen minutes –

DAN. Sorry –

CLAIRE. Is that a record?

DAN. Look –

CLAIRE. The phones are going mental.

Beat. The phones continue not to ring.

DAN. You must have been rushed off your feet.

CLAIRE. It's been brutal.

DAN. Look I am sorry –

CLAIRE. What happened?

DAN. I missed my train?

CLAIRE. Good one.

DAN. Twice actually –

CLAIRE. How do you miss the DLR twice?

DAN. There was this guy – and he had this dog –

Beat.

With three legs.

Beat.

CLAIRE. Is this a joke?

DAN. No – no, just my life.

Beat.

Did you um – did you – get back alright? Last night?

CLAIRE. Uh – yeah – all present and correct.

DAN. Good. That's – good.

CLAIRE *smiles at him and goes back to her work. He starts unpacking his bag and then –*

It's just you didn't text –

CLAIRE. I thought you'd be asleep.

DAN. Not for a while.

CLAIRE. Right – sorry.

Pause. CLAIRE *is looking at an email.* DAN *carries on unpacking and then, oh no –*

DAN. And Señor Socks was –

CLAIRE. Hm?

DAN. Your cat – Señor Socks – isn't that his –

TWO   13

CLAIRE. It is yeah –

DAN. And he was alright?

CLAIRE. Yes – yeah, snoring peacefully, as always.

DAN. Great.

Pause. DAN *is setting up for the day,* CLAIRE *is looking at him and then –*

CLAIRE. I would have stayed –

DAN. Oh my god – no I didn't mean –

CLAIRE. I don't want you to think – it's not that I didn't / want –

DAN. No I know –

CLAIRE. I just can't leave / him alone.

DAN. Can't leave him alone at night.

CLAIRE. Nope.

Beat.

DAN. You uh – you said. Last time.

CLAIRE. Did I?

DAN. Yeah you – I remembered.

CLAIRE. Good work.

DAN. Thanks so much, yeah.

Pause.

CLAIRE. He's scared of the dark.

DAN. Really?

CLAIRE. Yeah – he gets really loud, the neighbours complain –

DAN. I always just thought it was because he was old –

CLAIRE. No, he's terrified.

DAN. Oh my god.

CLAIRE. Yeah – I took him to this cat psychiatrist – He's a Scorpio.

DAN. Is that – is that a job?

CLAIRE. Yeah – She did his horoscope too.

DAN. Oh – wow –

Beat. He realises she's joking. CLAIRE *laughs.*

Right – right, very good.

CLAIRE. I mean look, he might be, it's not like he could tell me if he was.

DAN. He'd be like – meow!

Beat.

CLAIRE (*delighted*). What?

DAN. Because – he's a cat so he'd –

CLAIRE. What would he say, sorry?

DAN. No, fuck you actually –

CLAIRE. No, no go on –

DAN. Fuck you – Right – Is the urn on? Do you want a coffee?

CLAIRE. Oh I um – I got you one, actually.

DAN. What?

CLAIRE. I got you one – I got you a coffee. From Moritz.

DAN. Did you?

CLAIRE. Don't be weird about it.

DAN. No I'm not – I'm not being weird – it's very nice of you.

CLAIRE. He asked after you.

DAN. Did he?

CLAIRE. Yeah he said – your friend Daniel is a coool guy –

DAN. Well that's kind of him.

CLAIRE. Very.

She slides the coffee cup over, suddenly feeling shy.

DAN. Thank you so much.

CLAIRE. Just a coffee.

DAN starts drinking the coffee and looks around.

DAN. Is anyone else in?

CLAIRE. Nope. Just us.

DAN. Oh.

They smile at each other. Oi oi.

Busy day?

CLAIRE. Uh – sort of, I've got a call with Mandy to go through this – you know the carbon-tracking report we got done?

DAN. For the Greenpeace pitch?

CLAIRE. Yeah it – it came back last night and it's – well it's sort of quite bad, actually.

DAN. Oh really?

CLAIRE. Yeah it's like – it's actually sort of terrible?

DAN. Why?

CLAIRE. The bags are – much, much worse than we thought –

DAN (*faux outrage*). No!

CLAIRE. I know!

DAN. People love the bags, Claire.

CLAIRE. I know –

DAN. Donation model doesn't work without the bags –

CLAIRE. No, I know that –

DAN. No bags, no donations, no me –

CLAIRE. Which is what we're all most afraid of –

DAN. The new design is nearly out of stock already –

CLAIRE. What's the new design?

DAN holds a hand up – give him a minute – pulls a tote bag out of his desk drawer with 'Don't Be a Fossil Fool!' on it.

DAN. Activism!

CLAIRE. Oh god.

DAN. I know.

CLAIRE. But, Dan, like – if this is right, the suppliers have – basically they're using about twice as much water as we thought, and we were already pushing it –

DAN. Oh fuck, really?

CLAIRE. Yeah and the – well it turns out that actually the logos are not organic dye –

DAN. What are they?

CLAIRE. PVC – plastic, basically. So when that cotton has all rotted away you will still be able to see –

They both look at the slogan.

(*To an email that's just come in.*) Oh fuck off, Mandy –

DAN. Isn't it, like – four a.m. in New York?

CLAIRE. She's a vampire. She emailed me once at six a.m. on a Saturday – and then replied at seven asking if my phone was broken –

DAN. Jesus –

CLAIRE. Honestly she thinks she's played by Meryl Streep. You know she's flying over for this pitch?

DAN. For Greenpeace? She's flying over from New York to pitch to Greenpeace? In London?

CLAIRE. Apparently we're just not telling them.

DAN. Oh well that's alright then.

Beat.

CLAIRE *shuts her laptop: Let's stop talking about it.*

CLAIRE. What are you doing later? Any big Friday plans?

DAN. Me?

CLAIRE. Uh – yeah.

DAN. Oh – um – uh – no not really. Probably just go home.

CLAIRE. Sounds amazing.

DAN. You?

CLAIRE. I have to go to Simmons.

DAN. No –

CLAIRE. I know –

DAN. Who's making you do that?

CLAIRE. She's this – oh god she's kind of a friend? I know her from uni – it's her birthday –

DAN. Christ.

CLAIRE. I know.

Beat.

DAN. Actually – Claire.

CLAIRE. Yeah?

DAN. I've um – there's this really nice dumpling place –

CLAIRE. Loove dumplings –

DAN. I know – it's um – it's near yours actually?

CLAIRE. Oh really? Which one?

DAN. The one up by the railway bridge – next to the Lloyds –

CLAIRE. With the neon sign?

DAN. Yep –

CLAIRE. Oh that place is supposed to be amazing –

DAN. Yeah –

CLAIRE. It's really hard to get a table –

DAN. I actually – it's funny because I actually managed to get one for tonight –

CLAIRE. Oh – nice – just – just you or?

DAN. Well like it's funny you say that – I had to say that there was two of us to get the booking. So I – I don't know why but I said you were coming?

CLAIRE. Oh did you –

DAN. Yeah because – it was so weird they were like we actually need both names –

CLAIRE. Sure –

DAN. Which is a thing some places do –

CLAIRE. Absolutely heard of that before yeah –

DAN. So um – I mean technically –

CLAIRE. Technically –

DAN. Technically I guess – you could come with me. If you wanted to.

CLAIRE. Could I yeah?

DAN. I mean don't let me stop you going to Simmons with someone you hate.

CLAIRE. I don't *hate* her –

DAN. Sounds brilliant, really. Hope you get there in time for happy hour.

Beat.

CLAIRE. I could do dumplings.

Beat. He almost can't believe it.

DAN. Eight?

ANA *turns something on, it makes a low hum.*

Three

ANA. Nitrogen pull?

>EUNICE *looks up. Not quite at* ANA.

MALCOM. Done.

ANA. C-four – six-twenty?

MALCOM. Done.

ANA. Reading?

MALCOM. Thirty-one.

ANA. Hm. Down.

MALCOM. Yes.

ANA. Visible growth?

MALCOM. None.

ANA. Nano possibility registering at –

MALCOM. Forty – overnight high of – fifty-one.

ANA. Fifty-one, really?

MALCOM. Between two and two thirty-one –

ANA. Not bad. Salt level?

MALCOM. As programmed.

ANA. Great – and CO_2?

MALCOM. Um – rose overnight but stabilised –

ANA. By how much?

MALCOM. Nought-point-two over two hours.

ANA. So within the margin of error in the fen, that's fine –

MALCOM. We have – one set of germinated seeds left.

ANA. Yes.

MALCOM. I can work on extracting today –

ANA. You should.

MALCOM. And gel these ones?

ANA. Yeah.

MALCOM. Same sequence as before?

ANA. Let's – let's take out the Y-Fifteen on this.

MALCOM. Oh – okay –

ANA. Don't you think?

MALCOM. It's the only thing left to change, I suppose.

ANA. It's not in the water naturally and it's clearly not helping –

MALCOM. No.

ANA. And let's up the potassium –

MALCOM. Again?

ANA. What's it on now?

MALCOM. Uh – this batch was – nought-point-eight-one.

ANA. Let's do nought-point-nine –

MALCOM. Great –

ANA. And then – we can see.

MALCOM. Yeah.

Beat. ANA *is trying to put something back on a high shelf. Maybe we haven't seen she's pregnant yet.*

Did you try the / lines?

ANA. Yep.

MALCOM. All of them?

ANA. I did, yep.

MALCOM. And did you do the test –

ANA. I did do the test call.

MALCOM. And all –

ANA. All fine on our side – Fuck –

She loses her grip and the box tips, spilling black dust all over the floor.

MALCOM. Oh no –

ANA. It's fine – oh god – (*Shakes it off herself.*) Eurgh –

MALCOM. I'll sort it –

ANA. No it's my fault – where's the broom –

MALCOM. Are you okay?

ANA. I'm fine – where's the broom?

MALCOM. I'll – I can sort this out –

ANA. Just tell me where the broom is and I can do it myself –

MALCOM. It's – why don't you sit down?

ANA. Because I want to sweep this up.

Beat. A stand-off. MALCOM *gets a dustpan and brush from a cupboard.*

Thank you.

She gets down slowly and starts sweeping. MALCOM *looks at her anxiously.*

MALCOM. I really think – it would maybe be a good idea for me to –

ANA. I'm fine –

MALCOM. I just think in case –

ANA. God, Malcom, I'm not actually useless you / do know that don't you –

MALCOM. I didn't mean – I never said –

ANA. I am just pregnant I am not completely fucking incapable –

MALCOM. I – I'm sorry I just –

Beat. ANA *is suddenly aware that wasn't very fair.*

ANA. Malcom – I'm sorry.

MALCOM. I just meant – it's all over the floor and –

ANA. I know –

MALCOM. And I can clean it quicker – not that you can't clean it –

ANA. I know –

MALCOM. I really didn't mean –

ANA. I'm sorry for snapping.

MALCOM. That's okay.

ANA. I don't – you just – sometimes you can be quite –

MALCOM. I know.

MALCOM holds his hand out for the broom. ANA stands up, gives it to him and sits back down in a chair.

ANA. Thank you.

MALCOM starts sweeping. ANA rubs her eyes and starts doing computer work.

MALCOM. Did you know that eighty-six straight days of storming in this part of the world actually does make it a freak weather event?

ANA. What?

MALCOM. As of this morning we're at eighty-six days of storming over an eight on the Beaufort scale –

ANA. Eighty-six –

MALCOM. Making it a freak weather event. Which is funny sort of isn't it because we don't really – you don't really get those any more. Actually the last time there was a storm streak this bad in Svalbard was nearly fifty years ago – 2056 –

ANA. Was it.

MALCOM. That was before they moved everyone off – because people used to live here year-round – on the surface –

ANA. I know –

MALCOM. Feels sort of crazy now doesn't it – that people used to –

Wind wind wind.

ANA. Malcom –

MALCOM. Hm?

ANA. It will blow out soon.

MALCOM. Yes.

ANA. It has to.

MALCOM. Last year in Florida there was a storm that lasted for one hundred and two days.

ANA. That was – we're not in Florida.

MALCOM. By the end of it –

ANA. We are not in Florida.

MALCOM. I know.

ANA. It will blow out – and then the lines will work.

MALCOM. Yes.

ANA. And they will come and get us.

MALCOM. Yes.

ANA. And we'll go home.

MALCOM. Yes.

Beat. MALCOM *goes back to cleaning.* ANA *feels bad.*

ANA. Shall I – can I make you a coffee?

MALCOM. Oh – um –

ANA. It's no bother – I was going to make one anyway –

MALCOM. Oh um – no it's okay, I can do it –

ANA. Let me make you a coffee. You're cleaning up my mess.

MALCOM. I don't mind.

ANA. Let me – would you let me do it?

MALCOM. I don't – it's not – it's nothing, I can do it after I do this –

ANA. But I want a coffee now –

MALCOM. Then I'll – I'll do this later –

ANA. It will take me two seconds – I promise not to pour boiling water up my birthing canal –

MALCOM. Ah –

ANA. Do I make really awful coffee?

MALCOM. What?

ANA. You never let me make the coffee –

Beat.

MALCOM. That's not true –

ANA. Yes it is –

MALCOM. No it's / not –

ANA. Oh my god it is – it is true – I hadn't realised – you literally have not let me make one single coffee –

MALCOM. I don't think –

ANA. Every time I say 'oh do you fancy a coffee' you leap out of your skin.

MALCOM. I don't –

ANA. You do! Oh my god I make terrible coffee –

MALCOM. You don't –

ANA. Well you wouldn't really know would you – I think I maybe made one? And since then it's been –

MALCOM. It's really no trouble –

ANA. That, exactly.

MALCOM. I don't mind doing it.

ANA. Malcom. Can you just. Let me – do this – can you let me make you a coffee?

Beat.

MALCOM. Um –

ANA. Malcom –

MALCOM. Yes. Yes. I'd like a coffee.

EUNICE. John?

ANA. Amazing. That wasn't so hard was it.

Four

JOHN *is reading in a chair.* EUNICE *has poured two drinks.*

EUNICE. John –

JOHN. Yes?

EUNICE. I've brought you a drink –

She holds it out. Slightly baffled, he takes it.

JOHN. What are we celebrating?

EUNICE. To the – to the future.

JOHN. To the future.

They take a drink.

Are you – are we –

He gestures to her stomach.

EUNICE. What? Oh – god no – no, not that –

JOHN (*laughing*). God no?

EUNICE. No I didn't mean –

JOHN. You sound horrified –

EUNICE. It's not that – I'm not –

JOHN. I know –

EUNICE. I wouldn't be –

JOHN (*gently*). I know.

Beat.

So what is it?

EUNICE *takes another drink.*

EUNICE. I just – I had this – I can't believe I didn't think of it earlier –

JOHN. Oh?

EUNICE. Yes I thought – I thought god wouldn't it be – amazing, if I had a man's name, just a man's name to – just to submit under –

JOHN. A nom de plume –

EUNICE. So they'd read it at least –

JOHN. Oh, we could have some fun with that –

EUNICE. Then, John, I realised – well they'll never let me present when they find out –

JOHN. Ah –

EUNICE. So then I thought –

She takes another drink.

Then I thought what if I *was* a man?

JOHN. What?

EUNICE. What if I gave the research to a man I trusted – loved –

JOHN. Eunice –

EUNICE. They'd read it – they'd have to read it at least –

JOHN. Darling –

EUNICE. And because it's brilliant – you do think it is, don't you?

JOHN. I – yes I do but –

EUNICE. They'd want this man to present surely, in London – but then I thought well that's fine, I can just coach him, this man, he'd have to be clever to start with but that's fine, I know a clever man – and then when he does a brilliant presentation – which he will – because he's brilliant – then they'll maybe fund him to write a book and we could write it – I could write it and teach him as I went and he could take all the meetings and the tours and the press and the fame and I could do – I could do the work – I'd do all the work –

JOHN. Eunice –

EUNICE. I know – I know you get – the nerves I know –

JOHN. It isn't the nerves –

EUNICE. What then?

JOHN. I – it's not my work. I didn't write it –

EUNICE. But you could have –

JOHN. No, Eunice –

EUNICE. Yes you could – what about your inventions?

JOHN. My – they're barely *inventions* – I'm just tinkering –

EUNICE. I think they're brilliant –

JOHN. I don't think they're – I just want them to be useful –

EUNICE. They are useful –

JOHN. Eunice, stop it. I can't just –

EUNICE. Well I don't care – I won't care if they just read it –

JOHN. I think you will care – you might not now but you will.

EUNICE. I won't –

JOHN. Eunice –

EUNICE. Please.

Silence. It settles.

When I saw the thermometer rise I –

No one else has found this yet – no one. Not Joseph Henry, no one in London, in Philadelphia. Just me.

And I don't know – what it means yet but it – when I first saw it –

It felt like God was here, in this room. Just let me send it under your name. We can – everything else we can figure out later.

Beat.

JOHN. Did you really feel that? Here – in this room?

EUNICE. As clear as anything. Like he was standing next to me.

JOHN. What was it like?

EUNICE. Like I suddenly – like a fire on my face. Like the dawn.

Beat.

CLAIRE. You're lying –

JOHN. Alright.

DAN. I'm not –

EUNICE. Really?

JOHN. We can try.

Five

At the dumpling place, about half-nine.

CLAIRE. On the dance floor?

DAN. Right in the middle of it.

CLAIRE. Jesus / christ –

DAN. Everyone was looking at us –

CLAIRE. Oh my god –

DAN. Most embarrassing moment –

CLAIRE. Stop –

DAN. Of my entire life –

CLAIRE. She just like –

DAN. Shoved my hand right in there. Full tit.

CLAIRE. Oh my god –

DAN. People sat down to / watch –

CLAIRE. No stop – / stop –

DAN. So that's why I can never go back to Simmons –

CLAIRE. I mean yeah –

DAN. Genuine PTSD – flashbacks and everything as soon as I see the neon –

CLAIRE. Where did you meet her?

DAN. Hinge –

CLAIRE. Hiiiiinge.

DAN. I know.

CLAIRE. Always the way.

DAN. Like you'd know.

CLAIRE. I know things.

DAN. 'Oh I actually prefer to meet people in person.'

CLAIRE. Shut up –

DAN. 'It just feels more real – '

CLAIRE. Working though isn't it.

DAN. Dangerous though, dating at work.

CLAIRE. Is it?

DAN. Don't get me wrong, it's super-sexy until someone fucks it at the Christmas party –

CLAIRE. That feels specific –

DAN. I don't know what you mean.

CLAIRE. Why'd you leave your last job again?

DAN. Oh and that's the other thing – you're my boss.

CLAIRE. I am not your boss.

DAN. Think you sort of are.

CLAIRE. No, I checked, it's a diagonal line. On the company flowchart. Dotted too.

DAN. Sexy.

CLAIRE. Very.

Beat.

DAN. You probably could still fire me though –

CLAIRE. Here we go –

DAN. Which would be a terrible idea, by the way –

CLAIRE. Oh would it? What was it this morning? Sixteen minutes late?

Beat.

DAN. I can hear the tribunal now.

CLAIRE. Oh my god –

DAN. Hard-working, classically handsome employee gives his diagonal-dotted superior the best Thursday night of her life –

CLAIRE. Big claims –

DAN. She leaves in the dead of night to get back to a cat she claims is scared of the dark –

CLAIRE. I never actually said that –

DAN. Neither did the cat, / conveniently –

CLAIRE. Oh my god –

DAN. He, resolute and charming, takes her on a date, pays the bill –

CLAIRE. Don't be silly –

DAN. Pays the whole bill –

CLAIRE. Thank you –

DAN. A series of beautiful evenings and mornings pass – until she tires of him. Chucks him aside like yesterday's fish.

CLAIRE. Yesterday's fish?

DAN. Would you want yesterday's fish?

CLAIRE. Well – no –

DAN. Your Honour, she admits it.

CLAIRE. You are so weird.

DAN. Is it working?

CLAIRE. Yeah.

DAN. Good.

Beat. They really look at each other. Smiling. ANA *hands* MALCOM *a coffee.*

ANA. There you go.

MALCOM. Thanks.

CLAIRE. Do you want to come back / to mine?

DAN (*getting up to go*). Yes – yes I do. Yes please.

CLAIRE *laughs.*

Six

ANA. Thank you for cleaning.

MALCOM. That's okay. Maybe – / maybe –

ANA. Yeah –

MALCOM. I should do the –

ANA. Yep –

MALCOM. More of the – all of the carrying – because of –

ANA. I know.

MALCOM. I think it was fine before but I feel like maybe – the situation has advanced –

ANA. Excuse me?

MALCOM. With your – uh – um with us being here longer –

ANA. Do you mean I've gotten more pregnant?

MALCOM. I – yes.

ANA. Well that is – that is what's happened. I guess.

MALCOM. Sorry was that – should I not have said that?

ANA. It's just um – it's a funny way to word it.

MALCOM. I didn't mean to offend you –

ANA. No you didn't – just you know people normally say like – wow you're getting so big or – oooh any day now!

MALCOM. Right. Should I – say that?

ANA. I – if you want to.

MALCOM. I probably won't.

ANA. No.

Beat.

MALCOM. Are you – do you think about it coming early?

ANA. No.

MALCOM. I do.

ANA. I don't think it's helpful for us to / do that –

MALCOM. I've been reading about it a lot – since the storm started and you're – is it thirty-two weeks?

ANA. Thirty-six.

MALCOM. Thirty-six?

ANA. I think so, yes.

MALCOM. Oh.

Beat.

ANA. It's going to stop soon.

Beat.

MALCOM. Have you – given birth before?

ANA. No.

MALCOM. Oh.

ANA. This is not how I – personally – saw it going.

MALCOM. No.

ANA. I thought my mum would be around more, for one. My friends.

Pause.

MALCOM. I'm here.

ANA. Yeah.

Beat.

When the storm stops and they come and get us out – and I have my baby –

MALCOM. In a hospital.

ANA. In a clean hospital full of doctors. What are you going to do?

MALCOM. Oh um – I don't know really.

ANA. You're from London, aren't you?

MALCOM. Live there, yeah.

ANA. Right. Will you / go –

MALCOM. You're from Birmingham but you weren't near the fires.

ANA. What?

MALCOM. You said – a few months ago – you weren't near the fires.

ANA. Oh – oh yeah, yeah all fine. The fires were out in – do you know Birmingham at all?

MALCOM. No.

ANA. Right uh – well they think it started in the temporary housing up in Sutton Coldfield.

MALCOM. Right.

ANA. And I live in – miles away, basically.

Pause. ANA *might go back to her work; they both might.*

MALCOM. It's still scary though.

ANA. Hm?

MALCOM. When it's – when things like that happen nearby.

ANA. Yeah.

MALCOM. You feel like it shouldn't be happening to you. Like it's something that's supposed to happen far away. To faraway people.

Pause. ANA *looks at him.*

ANA. Yeah. You know the sky – the sky was so – it looked like –

MALCOM. I saw pictures. The orange –

ANA. It didn't look real, did it? It looked like – like a nightmare or – like – [*hell.*]

And for three days at the start the smog – the smog was so heavy that it was like the sun didn't come up at all.

It wasn't like normal smog it was – you could – it was like you could taste it. Even inside – even with filters you could taste the heat – the um –

The people. The –

You know in the old days you could outrun fires?

EUNICE. When I was ten.

ANA. On foot?

EUNICE. I went to London with my parents.

ANA. That's how slow they were.

The lights go off.

MALCOM. I'll check the generator.

Seven

EUNICE. My father was presenting – at the Royal Society.

ANA. Thank you –

EUNICE. The Royal Society. In London. Home of the Enlightenment – I was in awe.

My mother thought it was ridiculous to bring me – but he'd insisted. Weeks and weeks of travelling and we weren't even allowed inside to watch – she said I was too young to understand. But I knew – I knew what it meant.

The morning he was to speak, we walked with him over to the chambers, and I saw over the door – *Nullius in verba*. Take no one's word for it, Eunice. You must always, always question. That's how we make the world new, bright as the dawn. And then he walked inside – the door closed behind him.

We stood for a moment and then my mother took my hand – we had an engagement somewhere, some family member to see but as I turned I – suddenly I couldn't move – all I could think was –

I've been here – I've been here before –

It's strange.

Because I don't dream. Not really. Just one. And I've had it since I was a child. Every few months, the same dream.

I have been having this dream for as long as I can remember but I can't – I can never remember it's a dream.

And before that day, the day my father spoke at the Royal Society – I didn't know the dream place was London.

It is different in the dream, but the bones are the same, enough to recognise it. The Houses of Parliament, the bridges, the Thames. Except – in the dream, the Royal Society is opposite the Houses of Parliament. Which it's not, of course. Not far but not –

Even though I know the Houses of Parliament aren't opposite the Royal Society – every time I look across the street and I think – how funny. They must have moved it.

And it's hot in the dream – it's muggy – there's a sheen on the road like the air is broiling – and the road looks – funny – it's big and black and it stretches out impossibly far – and I can hear – there is a baby crying, somewhere close – a baby –

And there are – well I don't know I – they're sort of – carriages, I suppose – with people inside but there are no horses – and they are metal, I think – whatever they are, the road is crawling with them – dozens of them – jostling for space like ants – I can feel the heat kicking out of them – and there's no way to cross it so I am standing, looking out at the steps of the Houses of Parliament and wondering what to do – and then – from nowhere, there's this – this man.

This man – walking slowly up the steps – and he looks – his clothes are soaked, like he's just been pulled out of the Thames – I wonder if he needs help – and then one of the strange carriages drives past and in the second I can't see him he disappears and is replaced with a column of fire.

And then I realise he hasn't been replaced – he is the fire, he's burning, he's burning, and it's like – for a second it's like he's trying to scream – but his throat is melting – and then there is a crack, a shot, and he's down – he's still burning, he's still moving, thrashing. And suddenly there are these beetles – beetles the size of men glinting in the sun – I can feel their clicking through the ground – swarming around the man – I stumble backwards – turn around and –

The door has opened – the door to the Royal Society – I step through and it closes behind me.

Silence drops in, just for a moment and then – the baby again –

I can hear the baby again at the end of the corridor. I start walking towards it, and everything pitches to the side – suddenly I am on the floor and something is falling on my face – I reach up to touch it – it's – it's mud – no – it's peat, black peat is falling from the ceiling.

I get up and I try to walk again but it's like the air is molasses – and I realise my feet are – sinking in this pitch-black peat water –

But there – at the end of the corridor I can see tiny green shoots pushing up, growing in front of my eyes – and I feel this certainty that if I can just get to those shoots – I try again to walk but the water is up to my knees – and the baby is shrieking so loud, it's like it's inside of my head –

And I am trying so hard to move but I'm hip-deep in the black water and I look down and the baby – the baby – the baby is – inside of me and still screaming – pushing to get out – and there is another scream, a woman is screaming – and at the end of the corridor I can see a man and I try to shout for help but as I open my mouth the water rushes inside and I –

I'm awake –

Lights come on.

ANA. Thank god.

CLAIRE. Do you want a coffee?

EUNICE. I'm awake.

Eight

CLAIRE*'s flat. A few weeks later.* EUNICE *starts playing solitaire.*

DAN. Hm?

CLAIRE. We could go out. See Moritz.

EUNICE. I'm awake.

DAN. He'll be delighted.

EUNICE. I'm awake.

CLAIRE. Oh yeah?

DAN. He teases me about you all the time –

CLAIRE. Stop –

DAN. Always buying two coffees, Mr Daniel! And does she get you one?

CLAIRE. I will – / I did the other day –

DAN. You've got two years of coffees to make up for –

CLAIRE. Shuut up –

DAN. Adjusting for inflation / that's what – four hundred coffees?

CLAIRE. You get me a coffee like once a week –

DAN. And / there's the interest of course –

CLAIRE. And I don't know where two years has – interest! Please. I haven't even known you two years.

DAN. You absolutely have. I started June 2025 –

CLAIRE. Yeah but you didn't start buying me coffees the second you started at work –

DAN. No, no you're right there actually.

CLAIRE. Yeah.

DAN. I was completely terrified of you for about six months –

CLAIRE. Oh my god – you used to say good morning in this really funny way –

DAN. Don't –

CLAIRE. Like you were at primary school and I was the headteacher –

DAN. And then there was the – whose leaving drinks was it –

CLAIRE. Sophie –

DAN. Client services Sophie –

CLAIRE. / Bitch –

DAN. / Bitch –

CLAIRE. Fun night.

DAN. Very fun.

CLAIRE. Shut up.

DAN. But then you left like – straight away

CLAIRE. I don't think it was straight away –

DAN. I'm pretty sure I still had the condom on actually –

CLAIRE. Oh my god –

DAN. And you said it was for your cat –

CLAIRE. It was!

DAN. Yeah I know that now, but at the time it felt like such an obvious lie – and I just like – couldn't shake the idea that I'd upset you somehow so I bought you – a coffee – and you were like – This is the nicest coffee I've had in London – Because that was when you wouldn't shut up about living in Melbourne –

CLAIRE. Fuck you – / the coffee is different –

DAN. And you were like wow this is like Australian coffee where did you get it and I told you and then the next day you were in there when I went in and Moritz asked if you were my boss –

CLAIRE. And I said um – god did I say we were friends? And then he winked at me! Like legitimately winked at me –

DAN. I love that man, honestly. I think he might be my best friend. He invited me to his family restaurant, you know.

CLAIRE. Did he?

DAN. Yeah. In Bologna. He said – you eat for free – you stay for free – you just let me know.

Beat.

Kind of sounds like heaven actually.

CLAIRE. Oh yeah?

DAN. Simple life – rolling hills, red roofs – you, me, loads of pasta, help in the restaurant –

CLAIRE. I can't cook.

DAN. Oh I'll do all that – you can do – whatever it is you do now –

CLAIRE. I don't know how much demand for brand-to-brand PR they've got in rural Bologna.

DAN. Oh, of course – I couldn't drag you away from your true calling in life. Brand-to-brand PR.

She laughs.

CLAIRE. Maybe we start with a holiday, see how we go. I've got a week of annual leave left.

DAN. September?

CLAIRE. Go on then.

They smile.

DAN. Were you making me a coffee?

CLAIRE. I think I actually was offering for us to go on a lovely romantic stroll to buy you an iced coffee because it's one million degrees but if you'd rather have some steaming-hot Nescafé Azera then we can do that –

DAN. You can buy me a coffee if you want –

CLAIRE. Don't want to now actually –

DAN. Well I can't get you another one, the deficit is out of control –

DAN *spots* EUNICE*'s solitaire game.*

Is this a solitaire game? Do you play solitaire?

CLAIRE. Yeah –

DAN. With real cards?

CLAIRE. How else would I play solitaire?

DAN. On your phone? Like a normal person?

CLAIRE. Fuck off –

DAN. Oh my god we should play rummy –

CLAIRE. It is a Saturday morning and it is twenty-seven degrees, I want to go *outside* –

DAN. God you sound like my mum –

CLAIRE. Don't say / that –

DAN. Yeah maybe don't say that –

CLAIRE. And you were doing so well.

DAN. Do you want to go and get a coffee or shall I say something else off-putting?

CLAIRE. Ummm – No, let's go before it gets too hot –

DAN. Is that market on? By the station?

CLAIRE. Should be yeah –

DAN. God if only we had some kind of bag to bring things back with –

CLAIRE. I'm sure I've got one somewhere –

DAN. Oh – no need!

He whips out his Eco Market Solutions tote bag.

CLAIRE. Look at you!

DAN. Thank you, Eco Market Solutions – It's from when I started – look it's the old design.

The bag says 'Sustainable is Sexy' or something funnier.

CLAIRE. Do you know what – it is really nice that someone is using them –

DAN. People use these –

CLAIRE. Dan –

DAN. Why would they make the donation if they didn't want the bag?

CLAIRE. Oh I think they think they want the bag – but I don't think anyone actually uses them.

DAN. Number one: fuck you – number two: people use the bags.

CLAIRE *looks at him. No one uses the bags.*

ANA *spots something on her screen.*

Right, you can buy me a coffee and a fucking almond croissant –

CLAIRE *laughs.*

ANA. Oh fuck –

Nine

EUNICE *is working.*

ANA *goes over to the plants and starts doing stuff.* MALCOM *runs in.*

MALCOM. The emergency generator kicked in / but –

ANA. Power's gone off in the incubators –

MALCOM. Oh shit – sorry – [*for swearing.*]

ANA. Can you get the multifoil please?

ANA *carries on doing something,* MALCOM *runs to get the multifoil, and they start insulating the plants.*

How did you fix it?

MALCOM. I um – I didn't – the emergency power just kicked in –

ANA. Oh – good, that's – good.

MALCOM. I think there's a um – a leak maybe –

ANA. A leak?

MALCOM. Yeah – on the south side. There's a flashing panel –

ANA. Okay we can – we'll have a look in a minute.

MALCOM. I can go –

ANA. You shouldn't go on your own –

MALCOM. I think it might be getting / worse – out there –

ANA. Yes – yes I can –

Silence. The wind. Everyone looks up.

Jesus.

They keep insulating the plants. MALCOM *maybe wouldn't say this if they were looking at each other:*

MALCOM. When we go back – when we go back there's this café I'm going to go to.

Beat.

ANA. What?

MALCOM. There's a – when I – when we go home, I'm going to go to this café.

The wind.

ANA. Oh?

MALCOM. It's run by this Italian family – been there since the 2020s. In the evenings sometimes, when the heat has gone out of the day – when you can go outside, I like to go and have a cup of tea and sometimes, sometimes if the pollution is especially low they put tables outside on the pavement and I like to sit there and look at the city, at the people moving around. And I wonder what they do for a living and whether they're lonely. Sometimes they have chocolate cake there – not so often any more but I think – I keep thinking that the day I go back there it will be a cool evening and the pollution will be low and they'll have chocolate cake and I'll get a slice and sit outside. And watch the people.

Pause.

ANA. That sounds really nice.

MALCOM. Yeah.

Beat.

JOHN. Eunice.

EUNICE *doesn't hear him.*

Eunice –

ANA. Do your parents live in London?

Beat. JOHN *waves at* EUNICE. *She doesn't realise. He waits.*

MALCOM. Uh – no. No they don't.

ANA. Right.

MALCOM. They – we used to live in – near Cambridge?

ANA. Oh – I'm so sorry –

MALCOM. No it's fine –

ANA. Did they –

MALCOM. Um – no, not – no.

ANA. I'm so sorry –

MALCOM. It's fine –

ANA. I had no idea –

MALCOM. It's fine.

Beat.

They actually were very lucky – they survived the first set of flooding and – well everyone got put in this – well you know – camp. I asked them to move in with me but they were um – scared of being a – a burden, I suppose. So they said they'd wait and – they kept saying they'd be moved soon – they'd be assigned somewhere – they used to talk about the garden – having a garden again. What they'd plant. And um after – I think it was about a year, my mum fell on a walk and –

Do you know what a floating bog is?

ANA. No.

MALCOM. Ah um – they look fine on top but it's – she drowned, they think. She didn't come back. But um – it's a preservative, peat. When they found her it was months later but she looked like she could open her eyes. Like she was just joking.

ANA. Oh my god.

MALCOM. And then my dad – after they found her – uh – they think he – well they think maybe it was – because there wasn't a lot of disturbance – he hadn't even tried to – he just lay down. And sunk.

Pause.

ANA. I'm so sorry.

Pause.

Malcom. I'm really sorry.

MALCOM. No it's – it's okay.

Beat.

It's very common out there.

Pause.

ANA *pulls something out of her desk.*

ANA. Do you want some chocolate?

MALCOM. Where – what?

ANA. My uh – my mum got some – just before we came in. I've been saving it for an emergency.

MALCOM. Oh I couldn't –

ANA. Let's share it.

MALCOM. No I – are you sure?

ANA. Yeah. Yeah I'm sure.

JOHN. Eunice.

She splits a tiny amount of chocolate, they sit and eat it.

MALCOM. Wow.

ANA. Yeah.

Ten

JOHN. Eunice!

EUNICE. Hm?

JOHN. I've been – when did you get up?

EUNICE. About an hour ago.

JOHN. It's five – Liza hasn't even set the fire yet –

EUNICE. I just – I realised –

JOHN. Aren't you cold?

EUNICE. I thought, I was in bed and I couldn't sleep and it came to me suddenly, clear as a bell –

JOHN. You didn't sleep properly yesterday –

EUNICE. When the temperature rises –

JOHN. Or the day before –

EUNICE. If it rises in the tube then –

JOHN. Eunice.

EUNICE. What?

JOHN. We can't – we can't have this happen again –

EUNICE. Nothing is happening –

JOHN. This is three nights – last time you had three nights without sleeping –

EUNICE. This is nothing like that –

JOHN. I'm just – a little worried. That's all.

EUNICE. You don't need to be worried. Look, John –

She points at something in her writing.

When the air is damp like in the tropics – the sun has a far greater –

JOHN. Can you tell me at breakfast?

EUNICE (*still looking at her writing*). Don't you want to hear it now?

Beat.

JOHN. You shouted at the girls earlier.

EUNICE. I – did I?

JOHN. Mary was crying in the nursery.

EUNICE. I didn't –

JOHN. Augusta said you poured all the peat from their plant pots out of the window.

EUNICE. I – I didn't – I wasn't shouting I was just telling them – they didn't water their plants and now they're dead – that's what happened when you don't –

JOHN. They're children – they forgot.

EUNICE. I had plants as a child. I watered them.

Pause.

JOHN. They won't – they won't forgive you as easily when they're older.

Beat.

EUNICE. I do love them.

JOHN. I know you do.

EUNICE. I don't – I don't know how to –

JOHN. You do.

EUNICE. No, I don't – I don't know how to care about their – the things they care about –

JOHN. You don't mean that –

EUNICE. I do – I do, I don't care I don't – I don't know how I'm supposed to care that they lost a – a ribbon or a marble I – there are other marbles – other ribbons even –

JOHN. They don't know that –

EUNICE. But I do! I can't – stop – knowing. Just because they don't.

ANA is holding her stomach.

I didn't mean to make them cry. I don't want them to be – [*scared of me.*]

JOHN. Of course they're not.

The sun shines through onto EUNICE*'s set-up.*

Tell me, then.

EUNICE. What?

JOHN. Tell me what was so exciting you couldn't possibly sleep.

Beat.

EUNICE. Do you recall the pipes, what's in them?

JOHN. Tell me again.

EUNICE. This one has damp air – this one dry – and this one – carbonic acid –

JOHN. Smoke?

EUNICE. Smoke specifically from carbon – wood, coal –

JOHN. Right.

EUNICE. And look –

They look at the tubes in the sun.

– they're all the same temperature now, yes?

JOHN *takes a look.*

JOHN. Uh – yes. Yes, all the same.

DAN *is kicking his shoes off.*

DAN. Jesus christ it's hot –

EUNICE. Just wait.

Eleven

Throughout this scene everything gets darker and heavier, it feels like pressure dropping, like it's about to storm. It's about a month since their last scene.

DAN. Someone passed out on my bus –

CLAIRE. Oh fuck really – were they okay?

DAN. Yeah I gave her some of my water – she was alright –

CLAIRE. Hero –

DAN. That's me –

CLAIRE. Did you get the eggs?

DAN. Oh fuck me – no, sorry –

CLAIRE. That's okay, I can go –

DAN. No, no, I'll go back out –

He starts putting his shoes back on.

CLAIRE. Don't be silly, you just got in.

DAN (*big breath out*). God – sorry – I actually –

CLAIRE. It's so hot –

EUNICE. Look –

DAN. I feel like I've been sweating –

EUNICE. There, look –

DAN. Like constantly sweating for the last two months –

JOHN. Oh –

CLAIRE. Yum –

DAN (*smiling*). Oh yeah?

CLAIRE. Yeah –

Biiiig rumble of thunder. They all freeze.

MALCOM. I'll go have a look –

ANA. Okay just –

EUNICE. You see?

ANA. Shout if you need me.

ANA *paces for a while and then sits and starts playing cards.*

JOHN. I see. The carbonic acid – nearly a degree higher already –

EUNICE. It compounds. In the midday sun –

CLAIRE. Christ –

EUNICE. You can barely touch the glass.

DAN. Mum texted on the bus – it's pouring in Stratford –

CLAIRE. Oh yeah?

DAN. There's a flood warning actually –

He gets his phone out to show her.

CLAIRE. Oh really?

DAN. Yeah she's quite excited – says her garden really needs it –

CLAIRE. Her garden really needs a flood?

DAN. She's a funny woman – you'll understand when you meet her.

CLAIRE. Oh yeah?

DAN. Yeah – you know her favourite –

He's stopped by a text coming in.

CLAIRE. What?

DAN. Molly says it's – apparently it's really heavy, the rain –

CLAIRE. In like – a bad way?

DAN. I don't know –

Thunder.

EUNICE. I wonder if there is a level, if there might come a point where –

Thunder in 1856. They both look up.

Lightning.

DAN. Let me just call her quick –

DAN *starts calling his mum.*

The rain starts. EUNICE *and* JOHN *look out of the window.*

EUNICE. Look now – as the pressure is dropping –

EUNICE *and* JOHN *look at the contraption.*

JOHN. Remarkable.

CLAIRE *and* DAN *look out. Suddenly they look scared.*

CLAIRE. Oh shit.

DAN. She's not picking up. It's not – it won't really –

CLAIRE. No, no it won't properly –

DAN. She had – this is so ridiculous to say but she – she had a hip replacement a few months ago –

CLAIRE. She'll be fine –

DAN. But she wouldn't be able to if she needed – / if she needed to she wouldn't –

CLAIRE. It's just the heat breaking, it's always like / this in August –

DAN. I know – I know –

CLAIRE. It'll stop in an hour –

DAN. I know I just –

Thunder. Lightning.

Fucking – that is absurd – (*Laughing almost.*) That's ridiculous –

JOHN. You're remarkable.

CLAIRE. Do you want to go? And get her?

DAN. I don't – that feels insane –

CLAIRE. No, not if it would make you feel better –

DAN. Is that insane?

CLAIRE. No, I don't think so –

DAN. It's just her / hip –

CLAIRE. It's not stupid if it would make you feel better –

DAN. Let me – look, let me – I'll call my sister quickly –

CLAIRE. Okay.

DAN calls his sister. CLAIRE looks at the rain.

EUNICE. It makes you wonder –

Twelve

The rain carries on. MALCOM enters.

MALCOM. It was nothing – just damp – some water got on the sensor –

ANA. Great – thanks, Malcom – God I'm starving – are you?

MALCOM. Not really –

ANA. That's really woken my stomach up –

She gets a huge jar out from somewhere and puts a scoop of powder into a small bowl. She mixes it with the tiny bit of water left in her bottle and starts eating it.

Don't think I ate enough yesterday – I feel a bit – it's probably the caffeine, on an empty stomach –

MALCOM. Oh –

ANA. Just a bit – (*Flutters her hand over her chest.*)

MALCOM. Right.

ANA. It'll pass.

MALCOM. Have some – some water maybe?

ANA. Finished mine.

MALCOM. Have some of mine.

He passes her his bottle.

ANA. Are you sure?

MALCOM *nods.*

Thank you – thanks, I won't have much –

ANA *has a sip and passes it back.*

MALCOM. Can I ask you a question?

ANA. Sure.

MALCOM. Did you – did you know?

ANA. What?

MALCOM. When we came in – did you know you were pregnant?

ANA. Of course not.

MALCOM. Just that – if you're thirty-six weeks now – you would have to have been two months – nearly three –

ANA. I didn't know.

MALCOM. Okay.

ANA. That would have been against – you know that's not allowed.

MALCOM. I know.

Beat.

Because that would have been – that wouldn't have been – if you had known.

ANA. I didn't.

MALCOM. I'm just saying – that if you had –

An alert goes off. It's the emergency phone, they both recognise it instantly.

ANA. Is that –

MALCOM. Emergency line –

ANA *tries to get up but* MALCOM *is already running out the door.*

The siren gets quieter but it carries on, gets bassier and weirder, like something is starting to fall apart.

Thirteen

EUNICE. Do you see now?

JOHN. Yes. I think I –

Eunice, do you remember last week, when I was called in to the factory unexpectedly?

EUNICE. On Tuesday?

JOHN. Yes someone had – there had been some trouble, one of the women was injured –

EUNICE. You didn't tell me that –

JOHN. I didn't want to worry you – I wanted to see the new guards for the pressure rollers and to check that everyone had settled down – give the foreman some money for her.

It was a particularly warm day – if you remember – a beautiful blue day – and as I stepped off the ferry there was a particularly large cloud of smoke from the factory over the road and by chance it joined a particularly large cloud of smoke from the boat and for a second – just a second everything was white. Pure white. I couldn't see my hand in front of my face – like I was – like I was blind.

And do you know what I thought?

EUNICE. What?

Beat.

JOHN. Nothing. Not a thing. I just waited and – it cleared.

EUNICE *looks at him.*

EUNICE. What's wrong?

JOHN. I can't –

Beat.

Eunice, this is yours.

EUNICE. John, they won't read it with my name –

JOHN. I can't.

EUNICE. Why not?

JOHN. Because it's not my work.

EUNICE. I don't care –

Beat.

I don't care, John –

Pause.

I don't –

JOHN. I do though. I care. That's the – I care.

Silence. It settles.

EUNICE. Okay.

JOHN. Send it somewhere here – send it to Joseph Henry at the American Association –

EUNICE. I want – I don't want it there – I want it in London –

JOHN. I know – I know that. But to them it – they will never – you could have discovered gravity, Eunice, and they would insist they could fly.

But Henry is a good man –

Look I'll send it – I'll send it and I'll tell him I think you're on to something.

EUNICE. You really think he'll read it?

JOHN. I think he'll read it if I ask him to.

CLAIRE. What did she say?

DAN. Uh –

EUNICE. Alright.

DAN. She thinks we should go down there –

JOHN. It won't always be like this.

CLAIRE. Okay.

EUNICE. No.

Fourteen

DAN. She gets panicked –

CLAIRE. Your mum?

DAN. No, Molly – my mum's fine – she thinks we're being ridiculous –

CLAIRE. Oh really?

DAN. Mum said it's a bit of fucking rain – not exactly Hurricane Katrina –

CLAIRE. Incredible.

Beat.

DAN. It's fine though – it's fine isn't it –

CLAIRE. It's totally fine –

DAN. It's not gonna like *flood* flood –

CLAIRE. No – oh my god no –

DAN. It'll be like a bit of water – standing water –

CLAIRE. Yeah – It'll ruin her floors – she'll need a new carpet – that'll be it –

ANA. Malcom –

DAN. Christ, we'll never hear the end of that.

CLAIRE *gives him a hug.*

ANA. Malcom –

DAN. God I really –

ANA. My heart –

DAN. I really – freaked out for a second there –

CLAIRE. Of course you did –

ANA. Malcom –

CLAIRE. That's okay –

ANA. My heart is –

CLAIRE. It's scary –

DAN. Yeah –

ANA. My heart is –

> CLAIRE *does one of those 'in and out' breathing things. It's kind of a joke, kind of really nice.* ANA *does it too, she's really freaking out.*

CLAIRE. But she's fine –

DAN. She's so fine – Hang on – sorry, it's Mum –

> DAN *answers his phone.*

Hiya –

ANA. Malcom, I feel really really weird – Malcom!

> MALCOM *runs back in.*

MALCOM. I had them, I had them for a second and then the phone went dead –

DAN. Okay.

ANA. Malcom –

MALCOM. But they said the rain is due to stop –

ANA. Malcom –

MALCOM. They're going to come and get us / when the rain stops –

DAN. When the rain stops.

ANA. MALCOM –

Impossibly, the rain is getting heavier.

MALCOM. What?

ANA. My heart is – my fingers have gone numb – I can't get my breath –

MALCOM. Oh –

DAN. Alright.

ANA. The baby is kicking up – really hard –

MALCOM. Is it – oh my god –

DAN. If you're sure.

ANA. I don't know what's happening – I don't –

DAN. Okay –

MALCOM. Oh my god –

DAN. Love you.

ANA. Can you – maybe can you try and get them back on the line –

DAN. Yeah – I love you.

MALCOM. I – I can try but I don't think –

ANA. Can you just fucking try please –

DAN. Alright – see you in a bit.

MALCOM *runs out of the room again. The siren starts – stops – falters. It might come in and out.*

CLAIRE. What did she say?

DAN. They're going to get her when the rain stops –

CLAIRE. Oh right?

DAN. Yeah she says, they called, like the rescue – the fire brigade, I guess, called – and they said stay in place, stay on the second floor and they'll come and get everyone when the rain stops –

CLAIRE. Oh – amazing –

DAN. She says to stay put.

CLAIRE. Great.

DAN. There's – apparently they're putting in roadblocks – so there's no point me and Molly coming down –

CLAIRE. No –

DAN. We just stay put –

CLAIRE. Wait for it to stop.

MALCOM *runs back in.*

MALCOM. Nothing – just that –

ANA. Malcom –

DAN/MALCOM. They're coming when the rain stops.

CLAIRE. Yeah –

ANA. I know that, Malcom, I –

DAN/MALCOM. They're coming when the rain stops.

CLAIRE. It's all going to be fine –

MALCOM. I think it might be a recording it just – it just keeps saying that –

These lines should be quick quick – under each other, over the top, we don't need to hear everything individually.

Everything might feel like a nightmare.

CLAIRE. It's all going to be fine – it's going to be fine –

ANA. Malcom, if the baby comes –

CLAIRE. It's going to be fine –

MALCOM. It's not –

DAN. They're coming when the rain stops.

ANA. If it comes I need you to listen really carefully and do everything I tell you to –

CLAIRE. It's going to be fine.

MALCOM. I can try the line again –

DAN. They're coming when the rain stops.

ANA. Malcom, they are not going to answer –

CLAIRE. It's going to be fine.

MALCOM. The baby isn't coming –

DAN. It's going to be fine.

ANA. Malcom, look at me –

DAN. They're coming when the rain stops.

ANA. There's a baby – in here – I need you –

CLAIRE. It's going to be fine.

ANA. I need you to be calm.

MALCOM. Okay –

DAN. They're coming when the rain stops.

ANA. I know this is scary – I know – but I need you – to –

CLAIRE. It's going to be fine.

MALCOM. I think maybe –

DAN. They're coming when the rain stops.

ANA. And I think that / together we will be fine –

CLAIRE. It's going to be fine. / It's going to be fine.

DAN. They're coming when the rain stops.

MALCOM. Ana, I need to tell you something –

CLAIRE. It's going to be fine –

ANA. God it's like something is sitting on my chest –

DAN. They're coming when the rain stops –

ANA. I can't like – get / a full –

CLAIRE. It's going to be fine.

MALCOM. Ana –

ANA. Breath like –

CLAIRE. It's going to be fine.

ANA. Look – that's as much as I can –

DAN. They're coming when the rain / stops –

ANA. What if it doesn't stop? What if the rain doesn't stop? / I can't –

MALCOM. Ana, I've been giving you decaf –

ANA. What –

MALCOM. I've been giving you decaf. Coffee.

The rain stops.

Proper. Silence. And then –

Fifteen

Three months later.

JOHN. It's here –

EUNICE. What?

JOHN. It's here – the letter from Joseph Henry –

He holds it out to her.

EUNICE. Oh – oh you read it –

JOHN. Are you sure?

EUNICE. I can't –

He starts opening it.

JOHN. I liked him – when we met Henry I liked him –

EUNICE. He didn't say one word to me –

He's struggling with the letter.

JOHN. Well, you were in a mood the second we arrived at that dinner –

EUNICE. I was wearing that horrible dress – John, can you read it?

JOHN. Yes yes yes –

He gets it open. Reads it. He smiles at her.

EUNICE. Yes?

JOHN. They're going to publish it – next quarter. They're doing a feature.

EUNICE. A feature?

JOHN. They're doing a feature on – amateur scientists –

EUNICE. I'm not –

JOHN. You won't be – when they publish it you won't be –

EUNICE. I don't – / love that word –

JOHN. Eunice – you are going to be in the American Association for the Advancement of Science. You are an American Advancing Science – the first woman – this is amazing. You are amazing.

Beat.

You know, Henry told me at that dinner that science is the things in between the known. Science is in the gaps – what we used to think was spirits. You see them – the links – the missing things around us. You see some magic in a thermometer creeping up. As clear as I can see the sunrise you can see the golden threads that pull the world together. How beautiful they are.

And how beautiful you are.

We should go on holiday. We really – we should go somewhere. With the girls. Or we could take them to my sister upstate – go alone –

EUNICE (*this is exciting*). Just us?

JOHN. We could go to Washington – oh – no! We have to go to the Academy – in Philadelphia – And I can say – this is my very clever wife – she's in your latest – isn't she brilliant –

EUNICE. Stop it –

JOHN. And they'll say oh this is *the* Eunice Foote? We think you are brilliant –

EUNICE (*laughing*). John –

JOHN. And I'll say can you believe in London they won't even read her work –

EUNICE. Won't even read it!

JOHN. And they'll say that's Europeans for you – and I'll say that's why the smart ones all move here – there's gold in the very ground and even our wives can be scientists –

EUNICE. Even?

JOHN. Yes – even our wives. They wouldn't let you learn to read in England.

EUNICE. I'm pretty sure they let women read in England –

JOHN. Nope –

EUNICE. John, it's not –

JOHN. They lock them all away –

EUNICE. John –

JOHN. But not here. Not in America.

Pause.

EUNICE. I don't think I have time for a holiday.

Beat.

JOHN. What?

EUNICE. I don't – I think I need to work.

JOHN. You're being published – not everyone – you have done something amazing.

EUNICE. It is not amazing to me because I always knew I could do it.

Beat.

But I thought it might – I thought it might stop the feeling, but it hasn't –

JOHN. What feeling?

EUNICE. The need –

JOHN. What do you need?

EUNICE. I need to know – I –

She can't express it.

JOHN. What? What do you need to know?

EUNICE. Doesn't it drive you mad? Not to know?

JOHN. No.

EUNICE. Why not?

Beat.

JOHN. I want to go on holiday. I want to celebrate you. I want to wake up in the morning and for you to still be there.

EUNICE. I want –

JOHN. I want to look in your eyes and know you're thinking about me.

EUNICE. John –

JOHN. I am always, always thinking about you.

Sixteen

DAN *is wearing a suit, and* CLAIRE *is wearing a black dress.*

Two weeks since the last scene.

CLAIRE. Do you want a coffee?

DAN. No thank you.

CLAIRE. Tea?

DAN. No.

CLAIRE. Have you eaten anything?

Pause.

Shall I make you something –

DAN. I'm not really hungry.

CLAIRE. Okay.

Silence.

Do you want to practise your – the thing?

DAN. Uh – maybe.

CLAIRE. You don't have to – I just – when I did my dad's – I think it helped –

DAN. Yeah.

CLAIRE. It's – it is easier than you think it will be –

DAN. Is it.

CLAIRE. But it – you might feel better if you practise.

DAN. I don't think – I don't think I will feel better –

CLAIRE. I didn't – I don't mean better –

DAN. I know –

CLAIRE. Nothing is – nothing will make this better – obviously.

DAN. What's really mad is – I've been thinking about it and I think if I'd heard about it – if I'd just heard about this happening somewhere else I'd be like – all that flooding and only twelve people died that's amazing, that's amazing what an incredible job they all did – how *lucky* is that –

CLAIRE. Dan –

DAN. It's not like – not like a hundred people – not like a thousand – twelve people that's not even a Tube carriage –

CLAIRE. That doesn't mean –

DAN. Oh I know – I know but you know what I mean. Twelve people is a – a terrible sad awful day but it's not –

CLAIRE. Dan –

DAN. And I know that's an awful thing to say but I do think it's true – I don't think I'd have realised – if it had happened in Birmingham or something – if there'd been like fires in Birmingham and only twelve people died I'd think – got off lightly there, Birmingham –

CLAIRE. I don't think this is – a very useful line of thinking – right now –

Beat.

DAN. I just can't stop thinking about her sitting there. In her bedroom. Waiting. Listening to the rain – and thinking – they're coming to get me. When it stops they're coming to get me. When she would have realised –

Pause.

After my dad left there was a whole winter where I slept in her room. Because – because I was scared, I guess. I didn't really – I was so little I don't think I realised that's what I was doing I just – I wanted to be in her room. I wanted to be next to her. I'd open her door and stand there and she'd say – come on then – and I'd get in her bed and she'd give me a cuddle and I – wouldn't say anything.

I don't know why I never said anything.

CLAIRE. You were nine.

DAN. I just wish – I wish I could remember a time – I've been trying and trying to remember a time I said something –

anything – I don't know what I could have said but I want to remember saying something –

I think she thought I missed him but I didn't – I think I just didn't want her to be lonely.

CLAIRE. She knew that. She knew how much you loved her.

DAN. But I wish I could have said, then, that year – I wish I could have told her I don't want you to be lonely – even if that's not true – I wish I'd said it.

CLAIRE. Yeah.

Beat.

DAN. God. Fuck's sake – sorry –

CLAIRE. No no –

DAN. I just – I can't really – (*Laughs.*) I actually can't believe this is happening –

CLAIRE. No –

DAN. Like it doesn't um – it's just not something that happens – to you, is it –

CLAIRE. No –

DAN. It's something you hear about happening to other people and you're like Oh christ those poor fucks. It's not – it's on the fucking Central Line for fuck's sake – places on the Central Line don't flood –

CLAIRE. Dan –

DAN. I know I know I know this is stupid –

CLAIRE. It's not / stupid –

DAN. Did I tell you she's so bloated from the water they can't get her in a normal coffin.

Pause.

CLAIRE. I'm so sorry.

DAN. No – no I'm sorry that was – god – sorry – I feel completely insane –

CLAIRE. I think that's – I feel like that's – I think I'd be more worried if you didn't feel like that.

DAN. Well that's good. Very comforting.

CLAIRE. I try.

DAN. Thank you.

CLAIRE. What for?

DAN. You're being – you are perfect.

CLAIRE. Let's just get through today – yeah?

DAN. Yep.

CLAIRE. And then – well then it will be tomorrow.

DAN. Yeah.

CLAIRE. And we'll get through that too.

DAN. Yeah.

CLAIRE. I love you.

Pause.

Sorry that's so insane – that's such an insane thing to say right now –

DAN. No –

CLAIRE. Oh my god I'm so sorry –

DAN. Well don't take it back –

CLAIRE. I'm not – oh my god I'm not I'm – I actually can't believe I just said that –

DAN. Bit mental of you.

CLAIRE. Fuck –

DAN. Very clingy.

CLAIRE. Fuck off –

Beat.

DAN. Well, we'll always remember it –

CLAIRE. Oh my god –

DAN. Remember when it was my mum's funeral and you said I love you for the first time –

CLAIRE. Oh my god – I am the worst person in the whole world –

DAN. And then you made it all about you –

CLAIRE. Stop! Stop oh my god –

DAN. And then I said I love you too actually as it goes.

Beat.

CLAIRE. As it goes.

DAN. And actually I was so glad you'd said it because I kept nearly blurting it out.

CLAIRE. Yeah.

DAN. Yeah.

Beat. They smile at each other. Whoa.

CLAIRE. It's – it's going to be – it won't always be like this.

Seventeen

ANA. You've been – what –

MALCOM. I –

ANA. Malcom, it is really important that you tell me exactly what you mean, right now.

MALCOM. I've been – I'm really sorry –

ANA. Malcom –

MALCOM. For – since you told me, I've been giving you decaf coffee because I was worried that pregnant people aren't supposed to have caffeine –

Silence.

I thought it was probably for the best.

So this is – I think probably the first caffeine you've had in – about three months – which is probably why you're getting heart palpitations – and the dizziness – and the shortness of breath – you should drink some more water –

He holds his bottle out to her.

ANA. Stop talking.

MALCOM. I – what?

ANA. Stop it – stop talking.

MALCOM. Why?

ANA. I'm trying really hard – to be professional. But you are making it quite difficult.

Do you – Malcom, do you genuinely think I didn't know that?

Or did you think I was just a terrible mother?

MALCOM. No – no I didn't –

ANA. Pregnant people can have two hundred milligrams of caffeine a day.

Beat.

MALCOM. I didn't know that –

ANA. No, you didn't because you are not the pregnant person. I am. I'm the – And I am more than capable of not only doing my work here but also of deciding how much fucking caffeine is acceptable for *my baby* –

MALCOM. I didn't – I just thought –

ANA. Malcom, I don't care what you thought. Because it is not your baby. It is my – baby – and my womb – and my fucking coffee.

Silence.

Do you understand why this was a stupid thing to do?

MALCOM. Yes.

ANA. Great. Can you go and check on the leak please?

MALCOM. I fixed it – it's not flashing any more –

ANA. Then can you go and stand outside for thirty seconds?

MALCOM. I – Why?

ANA. Because I need you not to be in here for thirty seconds.

Wind rising. MALCOM *turns to go.*

MALCOM. I just – I was scared – I was scared it would –

Beat.

ANA. Yeah.

MALCOM. I'm sorry –

Beat.

ANA. Thank you for apologising.

Beat. MALCOM *goes outside.*

ANA *expresses her fury somehow. A moment, then she goes back to work, something with the samples, looks at some data.*

MALCOM *comes back in.*

It's not going to work.

MALCOM. It might.

ANA. No it's – it's not. We have done seventy-one batches of these seeds – forty more than we were supposed to and not a single one has – nothing.

What a colossal waste of everyone's time.

You know I really – I really –

Beat.

Do you believe in God, Malcom?

MALCOM. I – do I what?

ANA. Do you believe in God?

MALCOM. Uh – no – sorry –

ANA. Have you ever been in a church?

MALCOM. No.

ANA. I went in one once. My mum studied history – she's very into all that. She was doing our family tree – found this relative who was actually buried in one, well outside it but still –

We went in and – there's this huge window – stained-glass window, the afternoon sun is streaming in – and we walked up to the altar, where they would have done um – christenings – you know with babies? And there was this groove – on the steps up to the altar there was this – the step was worn away, not by wind or rain or – but by people's feet. By hundreds of years of people standing in the same place. And I felt this – I don't know I – I stood in the groove and I waited to feel something – to feel God –

MALCOM. Did you?

ANA. You know I started looking for this strain of wheat about four years ago – I'd been on this team studying wet farming after my postgrad and we'd had our funding cut – too complicated, not quick enough – but when the flood defences failed I thought – we're going to need to do something with – there has to be something we can do with all that land –

So I'm trawling through every database for every seed bank and I'm desperately thinking – clawing for something that might work and one day at two in the morning I come across this strain of wheat from a fen in New Zealand – and I look up the conditions in that fen and they are eerily similar to the conditions in East Anglia and I honestly felt –

She laughs.

I felt like the sun was rising right there in my kitchen. Like it was shining on my face.

I suddenly understood how they built that church with their bare hands.

But it hasn't worked – so that's –

MALCOM. It still might. It's why I applied – if we could do something useful with that land – where they –

Another blackout. A howl of wind and rain. ANA *unravels.*

ANA. Fuck –

MALCOM. I'll go –

ANA. I can't –

MALCOM. It'll just be the generator –

ANA. I can't –

MALCOM. / I'll fix it –

ANA. / I don't know how much – I don't know how / much longer –

MALCOM. It won't take me a minute –

ANA. Can't you hear it? Out there? Fucking hell, Malcom, can you –

MALCOM. It'll blow itself out. / It'll stop soon –

ANA. What if it doesn't? What if it doesn't what if it doesn't what if – oh my god what if we're just here and I have a baby – what if we're just – what if she's breech what if the umbilical cord is wrapped around her neck what if the placenta rips my insides out what if I bleed out on the floor what if I don't and then I just have a baby a baby and it won't stop raining it won't stop raining and there's a baby a baby a baby –

The lights come on.

MALCOM *and* ANA *look at each other. Maybe they look at each other the whole time until he needs to leave.*

Pause.

Eighteen

EUNICE *is reading from the article.*

EUNICE. This we are happy to say has been done by a lady –

JOHN. What?

EUNICE. The sphere of woman embraces not only the beautiful and the useful, but the true –

JOHN. What, Eunice?

EUNICE. 'Scientific Ladies'. That's – the title of the – 'Scientific Ladies'.

JOHN. What are you talking about?

EUNICE. There's another – they've published it with another experiment by another woman – it's not about my work.

JOHN. What?

EUNICE. It's about – it's about – it's a – curiosity piece. He says – in the – Joseph Henry – says 'though the experiments are interesting, there are many difficulties encompassing any attempt to interpret their significance – as is often the issue with hobbyists' – I don't understand what he means. He must have not read it properly –

JOHN. I don't understand –

EUNICE. Me neither –

JOHN. You have been published –

EUNICE. What?

JOHN. Joseph Henry has read your work –

EUNICE. And ignored half of it –

JOHN. Eunice, I told you they were doing an interest piece –

EUNICE. On amateur scientists, you didn't say it was –

JOHN. It was what?

EUNICE. About women.

JOHN. Well I – what did you think it was going to be?

Beat. The emergency phone goes off again. MALCOM *runs to get it.*

EUNICE. What?

ANA. Oh please.

JOHN. Did you – I didn't think – I thought that was –

ANA. Please –

EUNICE. No –

JOHN. Eunice, what did you think was going to happen? They weren't going to mention it?

EUNICE. I thought – I don't know – I thought –

JOHN. That's why they've published it – because it's incredible that you have the brain you have –

EUNICE. What?

JOHN. You have this – incredible – brilliant brain – in the body of a woman – that's remarkable – and this other woman must be the same, if you can believe –

EUNICE. What are you talking about?

JOHN. They're celebrating you, my love –

EUNICE. They're not –

JOHN. I don't know what you want, Eunice –

EUNICE. I want – I want what I've always wanted –

JOHN. Which is?

EUNICE. I want – I want to be taken seriously –

JOHN. They are taking you seriously –

EUNICE. They're not – they're not, John, I don't see how you can possibly – they've made me a sideshow –

JOHN. A sideshow –

EUNICE. That's how it feels.

Pause.

JOHN. I think that's ridiculous.

Pause.

EUNICE. What?

JOHN. I think you're being ridiculous, they have published your work, Eunice –

EUNICE. I don't care that they published it – I'd rather they hadn't –

JOHN. Do you. Do you honestly – do you really think if I'd offered you the choice you would have rather it be rejected outright?

EUNICE. Yes –

JOHN. Four months ago you were begging me to submit under my name –

EUNICE. I don't think I was begging you –

JOHN. Fine – sorry – that was – sorry –

EUNICE. I asked you –

JOHN. Yes – I'm sorry, that wasn't fair – but this is under your own name – your name – there in black and white – next to Joseph Henry –

EUNICE. I don't care – I don't care I don't care –

JOHN. You have to – you have to try to be fair, Eunice –

EUNICE. I'm tired of being fair –

JOHN. I don't think you've tried very hard.

Pause.

EUNICE. I – I am trying. All the time. I am trying – John, my entire, my entire life is – I feel like I have been trying and trying and none of it has ever made sense and it's never gotten better or easier or –

Pause.

I am trying.

Pause.

JOHN. I'm sorry it's all been so incredibly hard for you, Eunice –

EUNICE. That's not what I –

JOHN. I'm proud of you. Whatever that means to you.

Nineteen

They got home from his mum's funeral half an hour ago. DAN *still hasn't said anything. The wake was loud, the silence rings.*

CLAIRE. My sister sends her love.

DAN. Hm?

CLAIRE. She – she texted. Sends her love.

DAN. Right.

CLAIRE. Says we could go and stay at hers for a bit – like a weekend or something.

Beat.

Dan?

DAN. Yeah – yeah that would be nice.

CLAIRE. Bit of a / break –

DAN. That was so weird. Wasn't that so weird?

CLAIRE. I – it was – a really nice service. You were really good.

DAN. Thanks.

CLAIRE. I've never seen a church that full before.

DAN. Dinner lady.

CLAIRE. What?

DAN. She was a dinner lady – at my old school.

CLAIRE. Oh – right.

DAN. And she did the um – the choir, at church.

CLAIRE. That song they did was really lovely.

DAN. Molly picked.

CLAIRE. I hadn't heard it before.

DAN. 'God Be in My Head'.

CLAIRE. What?

DAN. It's from a prayer – the song – God be in my head and in my understanding; God be in my eyes, and in my looking; God be in my mouth, and in my speaking; God be in my heart, and in my thinking; God be at my end, and at my departing.

CLAIRE. That's beautiful.

DAN. She liked it.

CLAIRE. Was she – very –

DAN. Yeah. She was.

Beat.

CLAIRE. I was talking to some of the people from the food bank –

DAN. Oh yeah?

CLAIRE. This guy Henry – said there was one day a few months ago when they had all this food and it was about to go out of date – and she drove around for five hours dropping it off at people's houses –

DAN. They all do that.

CLAIRE. I think it's amazing.

DAN. It's what they do.

Beat.

CLAIRE. And the vicar said there was a garden – community garden thing she did?

DAN. Sometimes.

CLAIRE. Said she was there every week.

DAN. She was not.

CLAIRE. What are you doing?

DAN. What?

CLAIRE. What is this – thing you're doing?

DAN. I'm not doing anything.

CLAIRE. Okay.

Beat.

I'm going to make you a cup of / tea –

DAN. She was – she was amazing, she was but she was – she wasn't – the way they were all talking about her –

CLAIRE. Everyone was just / trying to be –

DAN. I know –

CLAIRE. No one ever knows what to say do they –

DAN. And that's the really funny thing, isn't it – that we're all sitting there talking about how brilliant she was and no one is saying that she / drowned –

CLAIRE. Dan –

DAN. No one's saying that she drowned on her own in her house –

CLAIRE. They told us – Dan, you called them and they told you not to – *she* said not to come – it happened so quickly there was / nothing anyone could –

DAN. I know that – I obviously fucking know that –

Beat.

CLAIRE. Please don't swear at me –

DAN. I'm sorry –

CLAIRE. No I'm –

DAN. You just keep doing this – this therapist voice and it's making me –

CLAIRE. Look I'm sorry – I am sorry, I'm trying –

DAN. I know –

CLAIRE. I'm really trying –

DAN. I know.

Beat.

This is just fucking mental, isn't it.

CLAIRE. Yeah.

DAN. Molly was sorting the flowers and she kept asking me what I think she'd like and I said I think she'd like to not be dead – and Molly looked at me and I felt this – unbearable shame – and I said I'm sorry I didn't mean to say that – and she said we just had to get through it and I thought – I don't know when she got so – she's so grown up. And she's been so amazing – sorted all the food and everything with the choir – she's had everyone staying in her flat –

I'm not – I don't mean to keep –

CLAIRE. It's okay –

DAN. It's just this – I keep getting this wave of like – it's not even a wave it's a – it's like – it's like there's two of me in my head – and one of me is – is trying to get on with stuff and is – thinking about flowers and catering and what prayers to do and who I still need to call and what I need to say and that I need to email the insurance people again – and then the other one is just – just screaming. All the time – and I can't always hear him but sometimes it slips and there it is again –

Maybe DAN *screams. Maybe not.*

And I kept having this thought today of like – like she's amazing, she was amazing – but she was – she could be hard, you know. She could be really fucking tough sometimes.

When she had to do that driving around – you know what Henry was telling you about? What he didn't tell you was the half-an-hour phone call they had where she called him a fucking useless idiot for not checking the use-by dates before he accepted the delivery.

And she would always pretend she didn't speak English when people asked for directions – and she fucking hated French people – and buskers – and once when I was nine she washed my mouth out with soap.

Maybe DAN *starts laughing.*

God I – I forgot about that. She literally washed my mouth out with soap because I – I'd learnt the word cunt from some kid in my class and I thought it was brilliant – thought it was so funny – and I kept saying it, all the time, and she kept saying 'Daniel that's not a nice word, we don't use that word' but I kept saying it and – I guess one day she was just really tired and she dragged me to the bathroom and she washed my mouth out with soap – and I was crying and then she started crying and she was saying sorry I'm so sorry – I didn't mean to do that I'm so sorry –

And she's crying – and I've got all soap in my mouth and I'm crying too and she's apologising and we're sitting on the floor in the bathroom like holding each other and crying – and it's all because I kept calling her a cunt in my tiny little nine-year-old voice.

Maybe DAN *and* CLAIRE *are both laughing by the end of it.*

That's mad though, isn't it. You can be – perfect, for so much of the time, and your kid is always gonna remember the one time you were sick and tired of being called a cunt.

Beat.

What's your mum like?

CLAIRE. What?

DAN. I don't know anything about her.

CLAIRE. I really – we don't have to talk about this now.

DAN. I've spent all day talking about mine.

CLAIRE. Oh she's – I don't know. She's um –

DAN. She's what?

CLAIRE. We just don't get on. I don't know – she was hard on us, when we were younger. And I never – I – I never really felt like she was on my side.

Beat.

She's a good person. She's just not really a – I don't know if she even – sometimes I think if she'd been born five, ten years later – she wouldn't have had us. And she'd have been really happy.

DAN. What makes you think that?

CLAIRE. I mean – lots of stuff really. How she talks about her life before – how she talks about when we were little. How much happier she was when we moved out.

There's this look she gets on her face sometimes.

Like she's looking at another life.

Beat.

DAN. Do you – how do you feel – about kids?

Beat.

CLAIRE. Positive.

DAN. Generally, or specifically?

CLAIRE. Specifically, I think. You?

DAN. Yeah. Obviously, yeah.

CLAIRE. I – I was always a bit ambivalent and then – oh my god – promise you won't laugh?

DAN. I promise.

Beat.

CLAIRE. I had this dream.

DAN. Come on.

CLAIRE. No seriously – seriously I had this dream like – two years ago – and in the dream I was pregnant and I – I was so excited, I was so – in the dream I was like – just so excited to meet her, the baby – and I – want to meet her. I want to know what she's like.

DAN. Two years ago?

CLAIRE. Yeah?

DAN. Like, when we met, two years ago?

CLAIRE. Oh my *god* –

DAN. Subconsciously knew I was the one before you did –

She laughs.

CLAIRE. Yeah – yeah that was probably it.

Beat.

DAN. I think we have them out of London.

CLAIRE. Oh yeah?

DAN. Yeah. Wouldn't it be – wouldn't it be amazing if they could like – swim in a lake and – climb trees and – if they could always see the stars – like how you can really really see the stars in the countryside.

Maybe we just fuck it all off and move to like – the Lake District, or something.

CLAIRE. The Lake District?

DAN. What?

CLAIRE. Have you ever been to the Lake District?

DAN. Yes, actually. Have you?

CLAIRE. I – no, I haven't.

DAN. Oh it's great – loads of lakes –

CLAIRE. Is it, yeah?

DAN. We could get a cottage.

CLAIRE. A cottage?

DAN. I mean for what you're paying here we could probably get a manor –

CLAIRE. With a swimming pool –

DAN. Tennis courts –

CLAIRE. Cinema room –

DAN. Good schools up there, I bet.

CLAIRE. That's a very grown-up thing to say.

DAN. Was it hot?

CLAIRE. Little bit.

Pause.

I could move to the Lake District.

DAN. Yeah?

CLAIRE. Yeah – somewhere quiet and – green. It sounds nice.

DAN. One thing we have to remember –

CLAIRE. What's that?

DAN. They have shit coffee up there.

CLAIRE. We'll just bring Moritz with us.

DAN. Move him into the spare room?

CLAIRE. I was actually thinking he'd come in our room –

DAN. Oh of course –

CLAIRE. Like if anything, maybe you could go in the spare room?

DAN. No, that makes sense –

CLAIRE. It feels more right I think –

DAN. No absolutely.

Pause.

I love you.

CLAIRE. I love you too.

DAN. Thank you. For –

CLAIRE. That's okay.

They smile at each other.

DAN. I'm excited.

CLAIRE. What for?

DAN. I dunno. All of it.

Twenty

MALCOM (*offstage*). *Ana –*

ANA (*jumping up*). *What –* what – are you hurt?

MALCOM *is laughing.*

MALCOM. *The rain –*

ANA. *What?*

MALCOM *appears. He is beaming.*

MALCOM. It's stopped – it's stopped on the mainland – the rain has stopped.

ANA (*sits back down*). Oh my god –

MALCOM. The wind is changing – they think tonight – they think they can get us tonight –

ANA. Oh my god.

MALCOM. They're going to ring back to confirm what time.

ANA. Oh my god.

Beat. They're going home.

MALCOM. I really am sorry about the coffee.

ANA. It's okay.

MALCOM. I didn't think about your feelings. I was just –

ANA. It's really okay.

Beat.

I did know. About the – I knew.

MALCOM. You did?

ANA. I did –

Beat.

MALCOM. Why did you –

ANA. Because I – it was only a few days before we came in and I – I knew immediately that I wanted – that I needed to keep her. I've never been – I didn't really plan to – I don't think it's very sensible. I can't – well I can't promise her any quality of life really. I have no idea – what kind of world she'll be old in. And I always thought – I couldn't do that to someone. But then I saw it, I saw I was pregnant – that she was a girl and I – god a baby – you know? A baby – my baby.

And I knew it was – I thought it was – I persuaded myself it was no more dangerous in here than it is out there – at least the air in here is always filtered – there are no heatwaves – no fires – no floods –

And it felt – knowing she was coming it felt more important to – try to –

But you're right, I didn't think about – I didn't consider how it might be – how it might affect you.

And I'm sorry about that.

Beat.

MALCOM. That's okay.

ANA. To be fair – I didn't think we'd be stuck in here an extra three months.

MALCOM. No.

ANA. But I am sorry.

Beat.

MALCOM. What's your – uh – her –

ANA. Her dad?

MALCOM. Yeah – what's he like?

Beat.

ANA. Uh – He's fine. I don't know – he's – I wasn't planning to have a child with him. But he can – he can be surprising. He can be wonderful, sometimes. And I think he could be a really good dad – if he wants to. But it's – I want to – you know. I want to be a mum. And that's – allowed, I think. I think I'm allowed to want things – to want that.

Beat.

MALCOM. I think you'll be really good at it.

ANA. Thanks – thank you, Malcom.

MALCOM *and* ANA *start cleaning and taking down their work.*

Twenty-One

EUNICE. It hasn't all been hard – or – it has been hard but it's not –

JOHN. It's all been hard?

EUNICE. No – yes – everything – always – has felt like there are all these secret – secret rules that everyone else knows –

JOHN. What rules?

EUNICE. The rules! How to speak and how to dress and how to sit and to talk to people –

JOHN. I don't know where this is coming from – I'm – I don't understand –

EUNICE. You are the most wonderful, wonderful man, John, and I love you, I do – but I am not – the kind of wife, the kind of mother –

JOHN. What are you talking about?

EUNICE. I can't do it I'm not good at it – I don't understand it – it doesn't make sense like this does – (*Waving the paper.*)

JOHN. I know you can be – you can be a little – particular sometimes but I don't – I wouldn't want you any other way –

EUNICE. Oh that's not true.

JOHN. What?

EUNICE. That's not true, John.

JOHN. What are you saying?

EUNICE. If you could have a wife who – who wanted to go to dinner parties – and dances – who wouldn't argue – if I just woke up suddenly one day like that –

JOHN. Then I would have to throw myself out of the window and into the Hudson, Eunice –

EUNICE. John –

JOHN. I don't want – a wife like that. They are perfectly pleasant to speak to for an hour – but I love you –

EUNICE. Why?

JOHN. Why?

She decides to tell him.

EUNICE. When we first got pregnant I remember thinking – this must be it now. This will – something will happen and I'll – everything will make sense.

But she's just – I remember – looking down at her in my arms after – and thinking – she's just a baby.

Just someone's baby.

And she cries and she needs things and she is always always touching me and – and I love them so much, I do – they amaze me – every day I – and I try I do try but I know I'm terrible / at it –

JOHN. You're not terrible.

EUNICE. John, please – let's not lie.

Pause.

JOHN. You are not terrible.

EUNICE. I'm cold.

JOHN. And I'm far too soft.

EUNICE. No –

JOHN. I am. Your mother tells me so often enough.

EUNICE laughs.

So we average out – yes?

Beat.

EUNICE. Perhaps.

Pause.

JOHN. You are the smartest person I have ever met.

EUNICE. You met Joseph Henry.

JOHN. And yet he couldn't understand your paper.

EUNICE laughs.

I didn't know. I didn't know you felt like this.

EUNICE. It's not – all the time – when I work – I can put it out of my mind. Because here – everything makes sense – I can trust my instincts.

Out there – it is made so abundantly clear that everything I'm supposed to be able to do is – feels impossible to me.

But I truly – I truly believe that God put me on this earth, at this time, in this century of discovery, to do my work.

JOHN. I believe it.

EUNICE. And I love you very much for it. But it has been – it is very hard to be faced with the reality of knowing, truly knowing in my soul what I was made for. And that probably no one – other than you – will ever believe me.

And I have been facing it a long time – but sometimes it is –

Pause.

I have been so lonely. For such a long time.

Pause.

JOHN. I'm here.

EUNICE. I know.

JOHN. Just here.

Twenty-Two

CLAIRE *is telling this to someone she doesn't know.*

CLAIRE. When the inquiry came out – he took a week off work. He'd been doing really well – we'd gone on this – really nice holiday. We went to Venice – it was – like – a joke, how perfect it was.

He'd been looking after his sister a lot – helping with her kids. His rent went up so he moved into my flat – he seemed – it was an awful, awful thing that happened but he was really – he was coping.

He was an exceptionally positive person – I think it's really important that you know that – he was never – before – he was so sunny. He was really –

When he read the inquiry he – I think he was hoping for some kind of – I think at first he just wanted an admission of fault with the way the rescues were handled – but then he um – the house – the house she lived in – the house he grew up in – it was on a flood plain. Like just – a flood plain. And when they built the houses – in the sixties – they knew it was a flood plain. Obviously they didn't know about the – the river and the – sea levels – but they knew it was –

The council gave them planning permission anyway. And there's this whole – one-hundred-and-twenty-seven-page inquiry with no – no one takes any responsibility. And everyone says we're so sorry and how tragic – no one actually –

He was um – he was deeply depressed, at first. He couldn't go back to work so they signed him off with stress.

He couldn't speak – I'd try to talk to him and it was like he'd –

Forgotten how.

And then um – after a couple of weeks he started – he started obsessively researching – he'd always been – uh – conscious of the climate, I guess?

But not in – I don't know like – he had a keep cup, he used tote bags, he drank oat milk – but he wouldn't have – he'd never have gone on a protest or – and we used to joke about it, like – my boss used to fly over from New York a lot and it was – but he would have gone, if they'd offered him a trip out, you know?

And then suddenly – almost overnight he became um – completely obsessed. He quit his job – our work – because he said it – it was disgusting, what we were doing. Filling up landfills with tote bags people thought were helping – he tried to get a journalist to cover it but no one would. He wanted me to quit but I – we needed –

He spent almost all his savings trying to offset the carbon from the flight we took to Italy – and then he found out that offsetting isn't really – he said it wasn't real – it didn't mean anything. So then he quit eating meat – and then he stopped eating anything that was from outside the country – and he didn't want to wash – I thought at first it was – some kind of late response to the – drowning but he – he was terrified of wasting water he said – we're going to run out of clean water, and then we're going to run out of food – he wouldn't go on the Tube, wouldn't go on the bus – wouldn't leave the flat – stopped eating anything at all because he got – he would accuse me of lying about where it came from, even if he could see the labels he'd say – I'd changed them or I – I don't know –

He really um – he wasn't well.

But then there was this one day – I came home from work and –

Suddenly there is a full steak dinner with two wine glasses and a record player in the space.

Or not.

DAN. Hey.

CLAIRE. Hi.

DAN. I cooked.

CLAIRE. I can see.

DAN. I got wine.

CLAIRE. Oh.

DAN. Do you want some?

CLAIRE. Yes please.

He pours and they cheers.

DAN. To the future.

CLAIRE. To – the future.

They drink.

DAN. That's nice –

CLAIRE. That is really nice –

DAN. How was work?

CLAIRE. Oh – fine. Did you have a shower?

DAN. I had a bath.

CLAIRE. A bath!

DAN. With bubbles –

CLAIRE. That sounds amazing.

DAN. I'll run you one.

CLAIRE. That would be lovely.

Beat.

DAN. Do you / have a lighter?

CLAIRE. What um – what changed? A what?

DAN. A lighter –

CLAIRE. Oh – yeah –

She hands one over and he lights the candle, pockets the lighter.

DAN. What do you mean?

CLAIRE. You seem – you seem really –

DAN. Better?

CLAIRE. Different.

DAN. Not mental.

CLAIRE. Less mental.

DAN. Bit less.

CLAIRE. What – I mean I'm – it's brilliant, but I –

DAN. I've just been thinking about the future – about what the future could be like.

CLAIRE. Oh?

DAN. What we said – about moving to the Lake District and – having kids there –

CLAIRE. Oh –

DAN. I want that – I want you to – have that –

CLAIRE. I want that –

DAN. How many?

CLAIRE. Two.

DAN. Girl and a boy?

CLAIRE. Go on –

DAN. Girl first –

CLAIRE. Obviously –

DAN. She can play football and he can do dance –

CLAIRE. And they'll both do swimming – and tennis –

DAN. Fucking hell all right –

CLAIRE. What?

DAN. Country club over here –

CLAIRE. Fuck off –

DAN. They're expensive those clubs you know –

CLAIRE. We'll be alright –

DAN. No – no we won't.

CLAIRE. Oh really? Why's that then?

DAN. Because stay-at-home dads famously don't get paid. Which is a disgrace by the way –

CLAIRE *laughs.*

CLAIRE. Stay-at-home dad yeah?

DAN. Well you're not gonna do the PTA, are you?

CLAIRE. No probably not –

DAN. You'd go fucking mental –

CLAIRE. God can you imagine –

DAN. I don't want to –

CLAIRE. You're going to be an incredible mum.

MALCOM. Ana.

DAN. And you will be a brilliant, brilliant dad.

MALCOM. Ana –

CLAIRE. I'm going to be such a good dad that people will tell you how good I am to babysit.

ANA. What?

DAN. Whilst I'm like – covered in baby vomit and scraping shit off the car seats –

MALCOM. Look.

CLAIRE. And I'm like asking you where the baby bag is –

DAN. And I'm like it's where it always is –

CLAIRE. And I'll be like where's that then, babe –

Twenty-Three

The seeds have sprouted.

ANA. Oh my god.

DAN. I love you –

MALCOM. Yeah.

CLAIRE. I love you –

ANA. It worked.

DAN. I love you so much –

MALCOM. Yeah –

CLAIRE. I love you –

DAN. I really do – I really really love you –

CLAIRE. I – I really love you too –

   CLAIRE *can't see him any more.*

ANA. When did that –

MALCOM. I don't know –

ANA. Maybe when the incubator stopped working.

MALCOM. But there was nothing this morning.

ANA. I know.

MALCOM. I don't – understand how it –

ANA. But it did.

MALCOM. Yeah.

ANA *reaches her hand out, as though to touch the plants but stops herself.*

ANA. It worked.

MALCOM. It worked.

ANA. I can't believe it.

Can you um – can you go and run a sequence please? A full one.

MALCOM. Yeah.

He starts to go. He looks up.

Look –

ANA. What?

MALCOM. Ana, look –

ANA. What?

MALCOM *points up at the skylight.*

MALCOM. The sun.

They both look up at the sun.

CLAIRE. I woke up to the sun shining on my face – we must have gone to sleep without closing the curtains. We'd had – the most amazing night. We danced, we ate. We had a bath.

He was already up, I thought he'd gone for coffee, or something. He was much more of a morning person than me – sometimes on the weekend he'd sneak out and come back with two oat flat whites and pastries – he used to do this bit – this like snooty-French-waiter bit – and I'd be lying in bed and laughing and I wish I had known – I wish I had understood how happy I was in those moments – I wish I'd pressed it in a book and saved it – listening to him do an awful, awful French accent and smelling him on the sheets against on my skin, sun pouring in through the window, hands reaching out for coffee and kiss me – kiss me, you fucking idiot –

It's too much.

Sorry –

Sorry –

Oh –

I just really miss him. I miss him when it's sunny and I miss him when it rains. I miss him all the time.

And I wish I had known in that moment, that last sunny morning, that was going to be the last moment I didn't miss him. I wish I had – I wish I could remember what it felt like.

It was an unbearably beautiful morning.

EUNICE. I have the dream again.

CLAIRE. The morning that it happened.

EUNICE. After my paper is published, I have it every night for a week.

CLAIRE. He'd left a note on the table.

DAN. Sorry I took your bag. I love you.

CLAIRE. I called him – he didn't pick up. But it was my swimming bag he took – so if he was swimming, he wouldn't be on his phone. So I – I just did what I always did in the morning. I got up, I made a coffee, I sat down. I went on my phone.

EUNICE. And it's the same as it always has been – as it has been for my entire life – I step out of the Society and look out over the cavernous black road –

CLAIRE. I went on my phone and there's this –

EUNICE. And on the steps – the man –

CLAIRE. This video. There's this man –

EUNICE/CLAIRE. The man is on fire.

CLAIRE. On the steps of the Houses of Parliament – I think it's fake for a minute but then I realise it isn't and I don't want to see it so I try to scroll away but it's there again and again –

EUNICE. And I can hear the scream melting –

CLAIRE. I turn the screen off – push it away from me.

EUNICE. Like wax pouring down a candle.

CLAIRE. I don't want to see it. The doorbell goes –

EUNICE. The beetles swarm over him –

CLAIRE. It's two police officers.

EUNICE. The dread sets in –

CLAIRE. And they have my swimming bag.

EUNICE. The baby is crying.

CLAIRE. And I know – but I don't – I don't know – and all I can think is – I lent him my lighter, I lent him my lighter, I gave him the lighter –

And I know that's so stupid – I know he would have just bought one –

But how could he do that to me?

How could he do that?

EUNICE. I turn to walk into the Royal Society, as I always do –

But it isn't there –

CLAIRE. He took my swimming bag because it's waterproof on the inside. He took a change of clothes and walked to a petrol station and told them his car had broken down a mile away. He put them in the bag so people wouldn't smell it on the Tube.

EUNICE. It isn't there –

CLAIRE. He got off near our office and he got a coffee from Moritz and he sat outside and ate an almond croissant and drank his oat flat white and Moritz asked him what he was up to today and he said the world is my oyster, my friend –

EUNICE. I turn back –

CLAIRE. After he had the croissant he walked / to Westminster –

EUNICE. But Westminster is gone too –

CLAIRE. Got changed in an alley and walked to the steps –

EUNICE. Not gone – ash –

CLAIRE. He'd posted a manifesto online about what happened to his mum –

EUNICE. Rubble –

CLAIRE. About what's coming – what's coming all across London, across the country – everywhere that's next – about the fires in America and Australia and the crash in insect populations – the soil degrading – microplastics in the Himalayas – inside of our brains –

EUNICE. Suddenly I am – I am high, high above the city and I can see –

CLAIRE. It's going to flood up to Tottenham you know –

EUNICE. The fire burning – spreading –

CLAIRE. Tottenham to Greenwich and back out to Richmond –

EUNICE. Like mould across the city –

CLAIRE. Do you know how many people that is?

EUNICE. Out into the country –

CLAIRE. And that's just in London.

EUNICE. The fire boils across the oceans –

CLAIRE. After they left – I couldn't stop shaking –

EUNICE. It climbs the land and burns the forests –

CLAIRE. Couldn't stop thinking – thinking –

EUNICE. The Amazon, the Redwoods – / I can smell it –

CLAIRE. I can smell it – from here I can smell it –

EUNICE. Acrid at first –

CLAIRE. I threw up –

EUNICE. From the animals –

CLAIRE. And / then –

EUNICE. Then sweet like a bonfire –

CLAIRE. I watched it again.

EUNICE. The trunks and branches –

CLAIRE. The whole thing, the fire, the shot –

EUNICE. Thousands of years to grow and / gone in a second –

CLAIRE. Gone in a second –

EUNICE. And the oceans boil and boil and soon the glaciers –

CLAIRE. It feels sometimes like I will live and die forever in that second –

EUNICE. Melting, hissing, / screaming –

CLAIRE. Screaming.

EUNICE. And the water climbs the land –

CLAIRE. They took it down

EUNICE. And covers the ash of the smouldering forests –

CLAIRE. The video and his manifesto –

EUNICE. And the deserts turn to glass –

CLAIRE. Took it down for terrorism –

EUNICE. And it shatters in the heat –

CLAIRE. Like he would have hurt anyone.

EUNICE. And the shards join the great grey sludge that make up the whole world and the whole world is nothing – and nothing – / nothing and nothing and nothing and nothing –

CLAIRE. Nothing and nothing and nothing and nothing – Nothing happened.

Nothing happened after that. I couldn't get anyone to –

And I'm so – I'm so angry with him. For leaving me here. Leaving us in this mess.

He wanted to get people to listen – he wanted people to know, to really know what was happening and to hold on to it and for something to change. But people can't hold on to it – it's too big and too scary and everything else is too hard.

How can you think about flooding in three years when now is taking all your attention?

And I used to think I was the kind of person who could do something like this – who could turn something like this into – I thought I was a big person. But I am – like we all are – incredibly small.

EUNICE. / But I can hear it –

CLAIRE. / But I can hear it – I can hear it – the future – I know what it looks like and I know how it sounds.

EUNICE. The baby.

CLAIRE. Tomorrow morning I'm getting a train to Crewe and from Crewe I'm changing to Penrith and then a taxi is coming to collect me and taking me to a cottage in a village called Rosthwaite.

EUNICE. And I wade through the sludge – / I can hear it –

CLAIRE. I can hear it – and it sounds like birds singing – it looks like blue skies –

EUNICE. I pick her up – I pick her up and she smiles at me –

CLAIRE. It looks like the stars burning above me – like little fires in the night –

EUNICE. She smiles at me –

CLAIRE. And the night means there will be another day –

EUNICE. She holds out her hand –

CLAIRE. And another and another –

EUNICE. She hands me something –

CLAIRE. Until there has been a whole life of waking and sleeping, a whole life of morning and nights without him –

EUNICE. And then she dissolves –

CLAIRE. And the floods won't get us –

EUNICE. Disappears into a pile of peat –

CLAIRE. And the fires won't get us –

EUNICE. I turn over my hand –

EUNICE *opens her hand and a plant is growing.*

CLAIRE. And you will have soft green to play on – grass beneath your feet – and the stars above you.

I can see the future –

EUNICE. How beautiful it will be.

ANA. So – let me get this right – one time me and my mum went to visit the grave of my – my great-great-great-grandma, so your great-great-great-great-grandma – and she was born in the 1940s – '43 – maybe? And she grew up in Newcastle, she said she could see the docks from her bedroom window. And she lived to like – I don't know – she was old – at least a hundred.

And Mum told me this story – that her grandma had told her – at school she had to ask a family member about the greatest change in society in their lifetime – greatest development or invention or something – and asked my great-great-great-grandma, and – this woman was alive for the end of the Second World War – for man landing on the moon, on Mars – for the invention of the smartphone and the first AI – supersonic jets and nuclear fusion – she was there – they barely had radios when she was born. And her grandma – your great-great-great-great-grandma takes a second, she pauses and she says – she says you never see kids without shoes any more.

You never see kids without shoes any more.

And sometimes I – imagine knowing – knowing that your children will grow up safer and warmer and less afraid than you did.

I'm so jealous of that.

So jealous that sometimes I can't breathe I can't sleep I can't think of anything other than the fact that the future used to be beautiful and now I don't even know if it's coming.

I know it seems insane. To do this now. To bring you in – and I'm sorry if that's right – I'm sorry if –

I think about it – all the time – I think about you falling – about your body bloating in the heat, in the water – I don't even know what you look like yet but I imagine your death all the time. I think about you choking on smog from wildfires, I think about you burning up as you try to run away, I think about you drowning – oh I think about you drowning all the time. I think about you starving – I think about you gasping for water, for water that won't make you sick – I think about you sick and shivering and I can't do anything – I think about trying to hold you and feeling your bones through your slick skin – I wonder what it will be like when you're old. I wonder if anyone will look after you. I wonder what will be left.

But I think – I think I am happy to be alive. I think it is worth feeling things like – summer evenings and a cold glass of water after a long walk and watching people opening presents you bought them and opening the door to your house and knowing someone else is in there and they have made you dinner.

(*Like she doesn't believe it. But she has to.*) There are still beautiful things. And they're all yours. I promise.

www.nickhernbooks.co.uk

@nickhernbooks